A Systems Approach
to Quality
Improvement

A SYSTEMS APPROACH TO QUALITY IMPROVEMENT

William F. Roth, Jr.

Foreword by Ned Hamson

New York
Westport, Connecticut
London

Library of Congress Cataloging-in-Publication Data

Roth, William F.
    A systems approach to quality improvement / William F. Roth, Jr. ;
foreword by Ned Hamson.
       p. cm.
    Includes bibliographical references and index.
    ISBN 0-275-94107-8 (alk. paper)
    1. Production management—Quality control. 2. Quality control.
I. Title.
    TS156.R674   1992
    658.5′62—dc20   91-4204

British Library Cataloguing in Publication Data is available.

Library of Congress Catalog Card Number: 91-4204
ISBN: 0-275-94107-8

First published in 1992

Praeger Publishers, One Madison Avenue, New York, NY 10010
An imprint of Greenwood Publishing Group, Inc.

Printed in the United States of America

∞™

The paper used in this book complies with the Permanent
Paper Standard issued by the National Information Standards
Organization (Z39.48–1984).

10 9 8 7 6 5 4 3 2 1

To my uncle, Fred Roth, with affection and respect, in thanks for the many contributions he has made to both my professional life and my private life.

Contents

Figures and Tables

FIGURES

TABLES

Foreword

Recently, I was flying from the United States to Australia to give a talk about the trends in quality and participation in the United States. Since the cabin was pressurized throughout the trip, I assume that the ideas that came to mind were not due to a lack of oxygen, but to the enforced opportunity to reflect on what forces were behind the creation of a now 20-year-old quality and participation forest. While some argue and perhaps hope that this forest is simply a very aggressive weed and not the dominant or climax species, I began to see during that 17-hour flight that three positive megatrends are driving individuals and groups in society to nurture and grow this seemingly new way of managing and organizing work. I also remembered one negative megatrend that for a while will continue to retard the full establishment of the new work forest. The trends I discussed were accompanied with a final caveat—look for people, examples, and books that will help you understand and cooperate with these trends. And especially look for resources that will help you apply what has been learned to date about the trends.

The forest example may bring the cutting-edge metaphor to mind, but this doesn't really capture the problem and it implies that it is something to be sliced up or through. The problem for individuals and organizations is not so much to be on the cutting edge as it is to ride the wave. Those who can't learn or won't even dare to ride the wave of change will certainly be swept away by it. Just as gravity, the moon, the earth's rotation, winds, and temperature change all have an impact on the size of a wave or an ocean, the trends outlined below are those that are creating and driving the sea of change in how organizations (now and in the future) will successfully serve their customers and manage the people and processes who produce their products and services.

Low cost and high quality are no longer separate choices

Consumers now know that they can expect and demand both low cost and high quality. There is not much more to be said about this. Even if the newest electronic whiz-bang product costs $100,000 in its prototype run, we expect that it will only cost $25,000 and will perform flawlessly within a couple of years. And the year after that, we expect to be able to buy a clone at the same quality level for $12,000. This expectation, more than the open market, is driving all producers of products and services crazy and is making consumers happier each year. But these same consumers can get real grouchy when this price-drop doesn't happen. The expectation is so solid now that grouchy consumers assume that if costs don't go down, someone is fixing prices or is denying them the products or services for some illegal, unethical, or immoral reason.

The hard-soft technology paradox

Hard technologies will continue to advance at ever increasing rates. This hardly needs any elaboration. (My highly technical definition of hard and soft technology is as follows: hard technologies are machine-like things; soft technologies have to do with people stuff—ideas, beliefs, values, and the way people organize themselves to achieve goals.) Something new is coming along every day that allows us to do things faster and easier or that we couldn't do before.

The speed at which new hard technologies arrive, however, creates an expectation that there is a hard technology solution just around the corner that will solve soft technology deficiencies. It also leads to a desire to treat and organize people as if they were machines. Has not each of us witnessed the inappropriate machine automation of a process because someone couldn't figure out how to get the people process to work consistently or just got tired of trying? Or if you haven't, ask yourself why is it that the less-automated NUMMI plant often outperformed highly automated GM plants. Or why at different times in history were rebels with fewer high-tech weapons able to win over their "better" equipped opponents.

The slower rates of improvement in soft technologies will increasingly frustrate those who work on and in organizational systems. This boils down to statements such as: "If we can put a man on the moon, why can't we get our management systems to meet that level of performance?" and

"We can pick off atoms and spell out IBM with them, why can't we get workers to turn out consistent high quality and get them to show up for work every day?" or, "It only took 30 seconds to fax my order to them, but it took 20 days for them to send me the wrong part. Why?" This drives individuals throughout organizations to look for new or the "newest" ways to organize people. It also drives those who sell organizational kits or systems to keep inventing new names for their products. This contributes to an ever-increasing number of different kinds of acronym soup on the organization shopping shelves.

All workers from the board room to the factory floor or office floor want to have a say in improving their worklife and work processes

This is a democratic trend that is at work in every part of society. One friend puts it this way—"Even old style bosses don't want to work for old style bosses any more." Another friend who follows Edward Deming's approach very closely, says that "All Harry Hubcap cares about is management improving his two or three square feet of work space, giving him what he needs to do the work properly, and then letting him get on with his work." That friend is right until someone actually improves that work space and consistently gives Harry or Harriet the resources needed. After that, a good number of Harrys or Harriets—whether machine operators, clerks, supervisors, or vice presidents—will want to have input on the area outside of their work space. They will want to have input on how their company/ organization produces products/services for their community/ nation.

You may not be comfortable with this trend and may have many cogent arguments as to why it doesn't apply in certain areas, but it can't be denied. The people in Eastern Europe, Germany, and the Soviet Union recently proved this point. The Chinese will soon offer another proof.

The most wonderful and perplexing thing about the democratic freedom/ control of one's "world" is the same thing that is perplexing about quality—each generation will take a look around their world and then apply the principles of democracy or quality in a new way. Each time someone thinks that definitions of either general or specific quality and freedom have reached the limit of their breadth or depth, and thinks they can rest a while—they are wrong. This is what Tom Peters means by chaos and another writer means by our whitewater future.

The class/status system of the eighteenth century still drives people's views of what is the best and what makes for the "good" life

The quality of life of and material goods possessed by the elite/rich of the eighteenth century still form our view of the good life and the good person. Hence, we still confuse luxury and quality. Examples—if you are really a good and successful person: you drive a luxury sedan or sports car that runs well only when it is perfectly tuned (which isn't very often); you wear a very expensive and exotic fur or leather coat; and you regularly dine on filet mignon or at very expensive French restaurants. If you are in the radical chic, you may well substitute a good Thai or sushi restaurant for the French one when you are trying to impress folks not in your class/status.

While there are many other examples of this trend, just look at the things that working class people buy when they buy over their heads. After they have bought those things, the upper class/status people no longer buy them; they look for a new definition of luxury in goods and services to differentiate themselves from those of lower class/status.

Remnants of this trend still befuddle us and will for some time. I expect that as the other trends roll along, this negative trend will lose its strength. The immediate challenge for many organizations is to get clear in their minds that there is a real difference between luxury and quality. In the long term, the customer prefers quality over luxury.

As I said earlier, all of us should be on the lookout for resources that help us to understand and cooperate with these trends. We should especially be on the lookout for resources that give us practical and current advice on how to apply what has been learned about these trends. I would add one more bit of advice: look for resources that focus on what really motivates people at work, rather than what we think ought to motivate people or what common sense (accepted wisdom) says motivates people. (Remember that each generation will supply its own definitions for quality and freedom.) In other words, look for resources that exhibit uncommon sense.

Bill Roth's book will help you understand and cooperate with the trends noted above and does so with a great deal of uncommon sense that will empower you with a very practical set of tools and concepts for today's and tomorrow's definitions of quality. His uncommon sense advice in a number of areas will give you as elegant a solution to some of your problems as was Einstein's formula $E = mc^2$ or a concept as concise as actress Mary Pickford's advice, "You may have a fresh start any moment you choose, for this thing we call 'failure' is not the falling down, but the staying down."

Ned Hamson
Editor, *The Journal for Quality and Participation*
Association for Quality and Participation

Acknowledgments

I would like to thank four groups and one politician for their contributions to *A Systems Approach to Quality Improvement*. The first group includes the professors at the Wharton School who taught me my trade. The second includes the employees on all levels at "Core" Corporation who allowed me to practice it and who have contributed greatly to both my efforts and my ongoing education. The most important of these is Doug Ferguson, who helped develop the model presented in this book.

The third group includes the editors who have helped me gather and successfully present my thoughts. John Kalish, a former editor of *Pulp and Paper International*, happens also to be a lifelong friend. Thomasine Rendero, an editor with the American Management Association, published my first pieces stateside and has been continually supportive. Ned Hamson, editor of *Quality and Participation*, has given me lots of good advice and has shared many good laughs. Finally, Jim Dunton, my editor at Praeger, has unerringly identified the screws that needed tightening as we've put my books together.

The final group includes people who have cheered me on from the start simply because that's the way they are—Jerry Anderson, Eileen Tasca, Napier Collyns, Jim Ravelle, Omid Nodoushani, Hal Dolenga, Susan Schuehler, Susan Ferguson, and, of course, the members of my family.

The politician I would like to thank is Congressman Don Ritter, who asked me to serve as an advisor to the Republican Task Force on High Technology and Competitiveness and thus got me started on this project.

Introduction

A growing number of authors is addressing our current inability to keep up with the competition in terms of both industrial and societal development. Concerning industrial development, the evolution of U.S. management systems continues to lag, despite all the buzzwords flying around. Due in large part to this lag, we are also losing ground in the technology race. On the societal side, control seems to be slipping away. We seem incapable of adequately addressing the problems of drugs, crime, poverty, a second-rate public education system, a health care system that is depriving a growing percentage of our population of reasonable attention, and a government seemingly dominated by special interest groups.

Despite all the promise of this era, our quality of life, during both work and leisure hours, is deteriorating.

One growing realization is that the problems of the industrial sector and those of society as a whole are linked. The solution to one set of problems might hold within it the solution to the other.

In the industrial sector, we are involved in a serious cultural change effort that, in most cases, is not producing the desired results. One reason for this failure, which I present in my second book, *Work and Rewards: Redefining Our Worklife Reality*, is that we have skipped the first critical step—examining and updating the concepts upon which our current reality is built. In terms of the workplace these key concepts are "work," "technology," "rewards," "development," and "success." It turns out that our definitions for most of them originated during the Protestant Reformation (sixteenth century) and haven't changed much since.

Work, for example, is done to generate the resources necessary to improve our physical and, as a result, our emotional security. Work is sacrifice. We spend a considerable part of our lives doing things that contribute little or nothing to the development of our potential to gain the paycheck that allows us to spend our nonworking hours as we see fit.

Technology, originally a friend who helped us provide many of the ingredients of physical and emotional security, is now suspect. Because it costs less and is more dependable, because markets are becoming increasingly competitive and profit margins smaller, technology is currently replacing workers and robbing them of the opportunity to satisfy their needs.

The only important reward is money. The level of individual development achieved is dependent on the amount of money we have to spend on it. Success, therefore, is still measured in terms of dollars and the number of "impression pieces" that we can flash, for, with Madison Avenue's help, these pieces have come to indicate our progress.

These concepts all tie into the Protestant work ethic, which was of great value in helping to pull people out of poverty and building a strong middle class as the backbone of society during the Protestant Reformation. (It still is of value in terms of pulling people out of poverty.) Four hundred years later, however, this work ethic has increasingly become a barrier to the efforts of what is now an extremely strong and well established middle class to get beyond the task of establishing basic physical and emotional security and to realize potential so that people may lead richer lives and contribute more to society.

My suggestion in *Work and Rewards* was that we transform the Protestant work ethic into a more comprehensive development ethic. Work is fine, but there are different types, some more fulfilling than others. Get beyond the dull, repetitious, sacrificial types of jobs. Let technology, with computers in the lead, do these. Encourage people to move on to more challenging, more stimulating developmental work so that our quality of life, both in the workplace and outside, improves. Expand the reward system so that money becomes part of it, rather than the whole; so that work not only allows but encourages the development of individual potential; and so that success becomes a more meaningful concept for us all, one which is defined in terms of contributing rather than of "one-upping."

People I know who have read the book have said, "Fine, we like your 'new world' work environment that gives us increased control over our lives, that results, ultimately, in a healthier society. But how do we get there from here? Your new definitions make sense in terms of modern-day reality. But old habits die hard, and the ones you are attacking, like workplace politics and in-fighting, are very old and stubborn indeed."

A Systems Approach to Quality Improvement is a response to these issues. It addresses the nuts and bolts of the necessary change effort. It is a "how to" book. The first, *Problem Solving for Managers*, was a "what" book. It presented a history of the evolution of management philosophy in the Western world, modern-day trends, and changes that must occur in the future. The second book, *Work and Rewards*, was a "why" book. If we understand what we want and the changes we need to make in the workplace, why are we moving so slowly? What must occur on the most fundamental level to make real progress possible?

A Systems Approach to Quality Improvement, therefore, is my "how to" book. In it, I define a way to implement the changes outlined in *Problem Solving for Managers* and *Work and Rewards*. I describe, step by step, an approach that I believe will allow us as employees to break free from our stale Medieval mentality and regain control of our reality. I then try to show briefly how the results of these changes will unavoidably spill over into society and change that, too.

What I suggest, of course, won't be easy. This is shown by the case study presented. But if people believe the approach to be valid, it will eventually succeed. The main driving force in human beings, after survival has been assured, is the desire to realize potential. When an avenue opens up, we crowd eagerly onto it, even if we might have to double back continually, even if we eventually get lost.

Cultural change in the workplace or on a societal scale requires three key inputs: (1) up-to-date, pragmatic *definitions* of the key concepts upon which we plan to build our new reality; (2) a comprehensive *approach* suited to the involved change effort; and (2) a *vehicle* through which the approach and the desired changes can actually be implemented.

I believe that all three now exist and have been spelled out in sufficient detail to be useable. The problem is that we have not yet realized the value of the three individual inputs to our effort, and we do not yet understand how they fit together.

The approach that will facilitate the desired change in both the workplace and society is the systems approach to management. The systems approach is not new. It is basically a product of scientific investigation. Since the Renaissance and the beginning of what we call "modern science," emphasis has been on analysis. When analyzing, scientists break down the object or event under investigation and attempt to identify its parts. In identifying the parts, the investigator carefully studies them and explores the relationships existing between them. The belief has been that by understanding the nature of a system's parts, and the nature of relationships existing between these parts, the investigator can fully understand the nature of the object or event itself.

This approach was critical to the development of the physical sciences. For some disciplines, it was, in fact, the only feasible alternative. For example, because of the limitations of early technology and theory, astronomers were incapable of formulating an accurate overview of the system being explored. They had to piece together their interpretation of it from a very limited series of observations that revealed only random bits of the puzzle.

In terms of the workplace, this approach has been most useful with mechanical systems. The wheel and axle, the lever, and the inclined plane have been identified as the basic design elements of all machines. Different combinations of these have made different manufacturing processes possible. Modifications of these basic elements have allowed the design of more elaborate combinations. Understanding a mechanical process, therefore, comes from understanding what elements/modifications are involved and how they fit together.

Yet when the human machine operator is added to the equation, problems arise with the analytical approach. Initially, attempts were made to define the operator as just another mechanical element. Break the employee's physique and personality down into their basic elements. Identify the employee's work-related needs in terms of their elements. Identify the relationships that exist between those needs. Then define the most efficient way of satisfying the needs.

However, with employee or "social" systems, and with the "socio" part of sociotechnical systems, it has been discovered that the analytical approach does not work as well as with purely technical systems. First, social scientists have realized that any social system is more than simply the sum of its parts and their interactions. For example, any sports fan knows that a team is more than a combination of individual players and the mesh of their athletic capabilities. The team's level of play depends on player friendships, grudges, team pride, moods, what somebody ate for dinner, what the coach says and when, whether every player's shoes fit correctly, and how much it bothers each player if they don't. Effectively modeling such a system is impossible. Too many rapidly changing degrees of too many variables are involved. And as we all know, successful analysis usually depends on exact modeling.

The second reason that analysis does not work as well with social systems and the social side of sociotechnical systems is that, as we have insinuated, they are part of a larger system or environment that cannot successfully be ignored. The larger system helps shape the embedded system's behavior. In order to fully understand the embedded system, we must also understand the containing system. In order to properly evaluate the operation of a research department, for example, we must understand the company's research-related needs.

As a result of these realizations, emphasis in management philosophy has begun moving away from analysis toward "synthesis." Instead of always looking inward and breaking things down, we are looking outward as well and attempting to piece things together in the most effective manner. This shift in attitude broadens our perspective tremendously. During the long reign of the analytical approach, emphasis was on the questions "what?" and "how?" We asked what the system was supposed to achieve concerning relatively short-term goals and objectives, and then how to organize it most efficiently to meet our desired ends.

The synthetic approach, with its outward perspective, encourages us to address the question of "why?" as well. We are beginning to ask *why* widgets are needed, what their value is. We have learned that social and technical systems on all levels and in all sectors have become so powerful and so interdependent that even a minor shift of emphasis or miscalculation in one can precipitate a far-reaching, devastating chain reaction, and that such frequently innocent blunders can set us *all* back in our quest for a better life.

Partly as a result of the above realizations, the systems approach to management came into vogue during the early 1980s. Interest in it faded, however, before its true value could be understood and appreciated. One reason for its relatively short span of popularity was that too many people in both industry and academia saw it as an unacceptable alternative rather than a complement to analysis. They saw the involved relationship as one of conflict as opposed to enrichment.

Also, the systems approach went against our strong tradition of "boss-ism" and top-down decision making. It called for the free flow of relevant information and for team efforts.

Executives therefore found it easier to label this innovative mindset as esoteric. Discuss it in training classes and executive seminars. Bring it up during brainstorming sessions. But that's where things stop. Actual implementation on a corporate-wide basis would place too great a strain on the current operation and resources. Things are going well enough. Mistakes are too costly in an increasingly competitive environment. The risk would be too great.

Today, these rationalizations have lost their validity. Things are no longer going well enough. We are losing our competitive advantage in market after market to countries that have learned what we have to offer and have gone beyond it. As a result, we are now playing catch-up.

One product of this unappreciated decline in our preeminence is that we have plunged headlong into the quality improvement movement. The Malcolm Baldrige Award, for example, has rapidly become the most sought after success symbol in the corporate world. The movement holds great promise. Indeed, it holds greater promise than most people suspect. Why do I say this? Because it is the *vehicle* through which the desired changes that we have been talking about in both the workplace and society can be implemented. It is the third necessary piece to our cultural change puzzle.

Unfortunately, yet not unexpectedly, the quality improvement movement has fallen victim to the same deeply ingrained habits that thwarted acceptance of the systems perspective. We have proceeded to break down into its critical parts what must necessarily be a holistic, systemic effort and have focused our attention on perfecting those individual parts. We have looked inward once again, rather than outward.

What will save us in this instance is that the need for improved quality will not disappear. The competition will force us to keep plugging away until we get it right. Then, because a comprehensive quality improvement process involves every part of an organization, and is systemic in nature, the systems perspective will permeate the organization's culture, inevitably producing a reorientation of both management philosophy and practice.

Once this happens in enough companies, all three of the pieces necessary to our quest—the foundational definitions, the approach, and the vehicle—will be in place.

Currently, very few of our corporate and academic leaders are thinking about quality as the vehicle that can bring both society and individual organizations into the "new world." They are starting at the beginning, and necessarily so. They are focusing on making companies profitable, non-profit organizations more effective, and the workplace environment more agreeable to employees.

Once they have succeeded in the above tasks, however, they will most likely begin thinking about sharing the lessons that they have learned with the rest of society. Corporations, supported by unions, government, the education sector, and service organizations, will then assume the lead in our cultural change effort and will hopefully be committed and strong enough to keep us on track.

A Systems Approach to Quality Improvement has three parts. Part 1 lays out what I believe is necessary to a comprehensive organizational quality improvement process.

Part 2 presents a true case history of the development and implementation of the model outlined in Part 1 at a pulp and paper company that we shall call the Core Corporation. Chapter 12 is an idealization of what could happen—once the approach and vehicle have proven their value at individual units—on a corporate-wide and on a community-wide basis.

Finally, Part 3 discusses the three major obstacles to the organizational and societal changes that we seek, showing their interconnectedness and suggesting ways to deal with them.

PART 1

More than the Sum of Its Parts

There is nothing more difficult to plan, more doubtful of success, nor more dangerous to manage than the creation of a new system, for the initiator has the enmity of all who would profit by the preservation of the old institutions and merely lukewarm defenders in those who should gain by the new ones.
Machiavelli, *The Prince*

"Quality" has burst upon the corporate scene. Very few major firms have not invested in it by now. The nature of this investment, however, has varied greatly. Many boards of directors, CEOs, and quality improvement departments still think of quality mainly in terms of quality control—inspection, standards, statistics. A growing number is realizing the challenge to be much more complex than first believed. They have begun trying to define and to develop what is necessary for success. A few have reached the point at which they understand the need for a systemic perspective.

The systems theory of management is built upon the tenet that "the whole is more than the sum of its parts." This means that when all the necessary pieces are assembled, and the relationship between them is correct, the whole created possesses characteristics of its own that go beyond those of the pieces. For a quality improvement effort to truly succeed, such a whole must evolve.

Several years ago I was asked to advise the Republican party's Congressional Task Force on High Technology and Competitiveness. One of its projects was to develop a generic approach to quality education that could be used in a wide range of industries and communities throughout the country. My main charge as an advisor was to help define the model that this education process would push.

After talking with quality gurus and the heads of relatively successful corporate quality departments, it became obvious that, while everyone had good pieces to offer, very few, if any, had developed a truly systemic package. This, then, was the task that I set for myself—to discover what exactly a holistic approach to quality improvement must include. The results of my efforts are found in the following chapters.

A Systems Approach to Quality Improvement has been fostered by several other key inputs as well. One was my doctorate in systems theory earned at the Wharton School. My teachers there included Russell Ackoff, the world renowned developer of interactive planning; Eric Trist, who helped develop the concept of autonomous work groups in the coal mines of England and fathered sociotechnical theory; and Fred Emery, one of the deans of the systems school of thought, who has written more on the subject, both individually and in collaboration, than just about anyone.

Another key input has been my ongoing affiliation with Core Corporation, as the company has worked to learn what it needed to gain the desired results from its quality improvement effort. The Core Corporation was the first to allow the implementation of the model presented in Part 1. It did so in two of its largest mills.

Thus, the first section of *A Systems Approach to Quality Improvement* presents the results of this long-term learning experience. Chapter 1 discusses the steps usually taken when an organization decides to invest in quality improvement, the frustrations that arise, and how these frustrations can be avoided. Chapter 2 explores in depth the five integrated phases that must be part of any systemic quality improvement process and their relationships. Finally, Chapter 3 singles out the most important and usually the weakest of these—the vehicle emplacement or team building phase—and discusses the glue necessary to hold it together and make it productive on a long-term basis.

CHAPTER 1

The Learning Curve

GEARING UP

Quality has become a central issue in our business community. Most companies of any size now have quality improvement processes (QIP) in place. If these companies have followed standard operating procedure in their efforts, however, chances of long-term and frequently even short-term success are limited. A cycle that is not only nonproductive in terms of the desired results but that can actually negatively influence productivity has been set in motion and will stall or even eventually derail what is being attempted.

In order to explain the above observation, let us move through the steps usually followed when a corporation mounts a quality improvement process. To begin with, the CEO, or the head of a major unit, having read or heard enough to believe, and rightfully so, that quality is a key ingredient to the improvement of both the company's and his or her own fortunes, decides that it is time to get something started. That person discusses the decision with key reports to make sure that there is no serious dissent, then either staffs a quality department or assigns quality to an already existing one, usually production or human resources.

The next step is to choose a head for the new function. Companies lacking real commitment or with a lot to learn assign this full-time job to someone as an additional duty. In primary industry, the new head is frequently an engineer. In the service sector, it is a member of the human resources department.

Once chosen, the manager or vice-president of quality is excited by the opportunity presented. The position is new. What can be done, then, is supposedly unrestricted by tradition and regulation. Also, the quality improvement theme presumably enjoys universal popularity. The effort, therefore, should not be hampered by divisional or departmental boundary disputes.

The quality head, however, is also wary. Because the territory is new and the position is not part of any traditional career path, he or she is extremely vulnerable. The new arrival must make sure at this point of the support of top-level management. Too many quality improvement processes are started solely for the purpose of image. The marketplace is demanding increased attention to quality. Image-oriented corporate leaders consider it critical that their organization give the appearance of having mounted a serious effort. At the same time, however, they are not interested in making the changes necessary to the success of such efforts. Thus, the quality leader is responsible for creating and peddling the illusion of change rather than facilitating the real thing.

Other corporate leaders want improved product quality but, at the same time, don't want to contribute personally anything more demanding than words to the process. Changes in their own mode of operation are out of the question. They are far too busy.

In both of the above cases, the quality leader will become frustrated, will not produce the desired results, and, unless a master politician, will suffer careerwise. That person must make sure that corporate leaders develop a gut-level, rather than simply an intellectual, understanding of the changes that must occur in their own work life and in those of others. The process will not succeed if the CEO simply gives a blessing, then sits back to observe. Rather, the CEO must constantly applaud and show interest in employee contributions. Everyone will be watching. If the CEO shows any signs of flagging interest, the process will falter.

Top-level executives must realize that what is happening is not just a change in structure or attitudes but in culture. An entirely new way of operating will most likely evolve. This means that there is no quick fix. The executives must be patient and encourage others to be patient as well.

Finally, the quality head must make sure that the CEO understands that such efforts can be destroyed very quickly by traditional cost-cutting measures. Many CEOs believe that getting rid of "dead wood," or downsizing, must be a first step in a QIP. Improved quality, they believe, depends on creating a leaner, meaner business machine. The need is to decrease the number of management layers to improve communication and to speed up the decision-making process. It is to eliminate duplication of responsibility. It is to get rid of bureaucratic slowdown by subcontracting traditional staff responsibilities to external support organizations. According to their way of thinking and training, all of the above can be most efficiently accomplished by cutting employee numbers in various functions and on various levels.

When a corporation downsizes, one of two methods is generally used. The first is early retirement. Financial incentives are offered. The second method is firing. It is cheaper and more controlled in terms of the number of departures. Therefore, it is more popular. Whatever the technique chosen, emphasis is on speed. Let as few people as possible know what is going to happen. Then, when it does happen, get those who are departing out the door as rapidly as possible.

Many things antithetical to the mounting of a successful QIP happen when corporations decide to get rid of dead wood or to downsize. One is that employees begin hoarding information to increase their value. Both intra- and interdepartmental contacts dissolve. Employees also have less trust in the information they receive. Anything coming from top-level management is automatically suspect.

Communication also suffers. The rumor mill dominates. People are given responsibilities that they have not yet been trained to handle. They frequently have to learn through trial and error. Problem-solving efforts lack integration. Units tend to focus on their own problems, worrying less about the adverse effects that solutions might have on other units. Discipline either becomes more severe or disappears entirely due to management's desire to regain the confidence of employees. The training department is cut, along with everything else, so that, despite the extra load, job-related development pretty much comes to a standstill. Job security is obviously gone.

In essence, the workload is up, training and morale are down, and, to make things worse, the anticipated bottom-line improvement is short-lived. Suspicions are growing that the exercise will eventually have to be repeated.

Trying to mount a QIP in an environment like this is not only absurd but insulting to the employees necessary to its success. Job security has to be promoted by management as part of the deal if it wants to generate the necessary level of employee commitment. Instead of getting rid of employees, the trick, therefore, is to better utilize their expertise as both cost cutters and productivity improvers. A systemic QIP provides the necessary vehicle for this alternative approach. Once the process is under way, those in positions that prove not to be cost effective should, whenever possible, be reassigned rather than released. If it becomes obvious that fewer employees will produce better long-term results, the unnecessary positions should be eliminated through natural attrition or early retirement rather than through firing.

MEETING THE CHALLENGE

Once it is assured that corporate leaders are on board and supportive, the new quality head begins a self-education process. The latest books on quality, plus a few classics are read. Case histories from other corporations receive serious attention. Seminars on quality are held and, if the schedule permits, visits to ongoing, quality-related processes at other companies are made. But this isn't enough. The ideal situation would allow the new head of quality a *year* in which to learn what is necessary. Required areas of expertise include team building, group process, problem solving, trouble shooting, technical training, the use of statistical measurement techniques, organization design, strategic planning, and systems theory.

The rest of the company need not wait during this learning period. The new quality leader can begin the familiarization phase of the process, at least for upper-level management, by using speakers, films, courses, and so on.

In reality, most new quality department heads do not have a year to learn what is necessary, and, if they did, would not have access to the requisite educational resources. As a result, they focus on one or two aspects of quality improvement and hope that the rest will come. In the meantime, they have to hurry and get something started. Time is short. Other "rising stars"—division heads or staff unit directors—have not waited for the new quality head to take the lead. Instead, they have done their own reading and have begun organizing their own individualized efforts.

Upon hearing about this challenge, the new quality head might turn to the CEO to block it. The CEO, however, is not usually willing to stop such subversive activities. The board of directors is currently stressing decentralization. Emphasis is on giving as much autonomy as possible to the major corporate units, and the CEO does not want to set an undesirable precedent.

This can be another serious mistake. Too often, the result is a hodge-podge of fiercely defended, poorly integrated, partially developed efforts. Units are unable or unwilling to learn from each other and sometimes refuse to communicate—even though increased communication is a major process objective. The head of quality should be in charge of selecting the most desirable elements from various approaches to QIP and then integrating and implementing them, first seeking the input from others on all levels who will be affected by these decisions. Once the customized package is defined, the CEO should mandate that this approach will be adopted company-wide and that any adjustments to it must first be approved by both the head of quality and the CEO.

A second realization that comes fairly quickly to the new head of quality is that while the theory part doesn't seem that difficult, implementation is another matter. How do you develop the necessary level of understanding, the necessary sense of commitment in a work force of thousands? How do you even attract the attention of employees when most of them are already overloaded? Where in the organization do you start? How do you change management practices that have been in place for 20 years? What kind of training is necessary for such efforts? What process techniques are most appropriate?

The new head of quality begins to feel scared. People in the organization are expecting quick results but seem to have little idea of what is required to produce those results. The head of quality looks for outside support. Mail has been arriving daily from consulting firms advertising their approach and trumpeting their successes. The packages offered seem to fall roughly into four categories. The first can be labeled the "efficiency expert" category. Emphasis here is on quantification. Time-motion studies, flow analyses, and statistical control systems are among the techniques advocated. Members of this group usually have been trained in the decision sciences and other "hard" areas and use the names Deming and Juran freely.

The second category includes "employee-oriented" consultants. Emphasis here is on improving communication between individual employees, groups, and units as a means of generating the desired level of commitment to cultural change. T-groups, management by objective, management by walking around, labor-management committees, and quality circles are techniques advocated by this group.

The third category includes experience-trained consultants. It contains corporations and ex-corporate executives who have generated or have been part of relatively successful quality improvement efforts, and have decided to make money selling their new knowledge and skills. Members of this group, due to their understanding of the corporate culture, excel at selling upper-level management on new ideas and approaches.

Most of the above types of consulting firms offer incomplete packages that do not take into account the unique characteristics of individual organizations. While many such packages have some flexibility, the tendency is to force the company into a mold, rather than to take the time necessary to redesign the mold. Much money and effort are spent up front by such firms to convince the head of quality and his or her superiors that a good fit exists when in fact it might not.

I would label the fourth and smallest category the systems specialists category. It includes professionals who understand the technical, managerial, and environmental aspects of a successful quality improvement effort and how these must mesh in order to achieve long-term as opposed to short-term results.

The head of quality invites the firms that sound the most promising to meetings. At these meetings he or she quickly learns that, as a whole, consultants are extremely competitive and extremely noncomplimentary toward one another. Comparisons are difficult to make. Due to the quality leader's relatively limited knowledge base and lack of experience, it is frequently the firm that is best at selling, rather than the one offering the best product, that wins the contract.

In terms of cost, the head of quality often feels the need to spend enough to legitimize the effort. For large companies, this can mean as much as one million dollars up front. The consultant chosen, therefore, must be the right one, and from this point forward a good percentage of the quality head's time is spent on insuring that superiors, peers, and just about anyone who will listen both understand and appreciate the wisdom and virtue of the choice that he or she has made.

This often frantic public relations effort is facilitated by the fact that the first step in every consultant's quality package is extremely straightforward and produces extremely visible results. It is to familiarize employees with the need for improved quality, providing an accurate definition of quality and an understanding of what quality improvement entails. Groups of managers and frequently line-level employees are either shipped away to a conference center or invited into classrooms where they learn what the different slices of the quality pie represent, how their culture is necessarily going to change, how to interact more effectively, and a variety of problem-solving techniques.

During this time the head of quality receives the first quantifiable and displayable indications of success. The growing number of employees who have been familiarized with these techniques, and the growing number and variety of quality-related posters, slogans, banners, quotations, pins, paper weights, and calendars that are appearing in the workplace, can be pointed to as proof of progress.

Eventually, however, the quality head begins to worry again. Following the comprehensive familiarization and training effort, the next step in the process is to transfer what is being learned in the conference center and classrooms to the workplace in such a way that the bottom line improves. The head of quality is not quite sure how this will occur. Neither, it frequently turns out, is the consultant.

Reality soon sets in. Changes don't occur in the way the training notes say that they should. For example, while quality circles have been formed, they aren't meeting on schedule; or they are meeting, but nothing is changing in terms of work practices; or changes are occurring, but they are causing new problems. While everyone now seems to understand the need for measurement tools, efforts to introduce them are constantly being held up or frustrated. While all managers had agreed during their training sessions that hourly workers should take more responsibility for decisions in their areas of expertise, many now seem to be having second thoughts.

At this point, the head of quality decides that it's time to move on and give someone else a chance. He or she has worked hard to make a noteworthy contribution but doesn't want to lose touch with his or her original area of expertise.

A new head of quality is chosen and picks up roughly where the old one left off, introducing some innovations and deciding that there is a serious need for more training. And so the process moves slowly forward until at least part of the desired change occurs, or until it becomes too expensive and a vice-president with a financial background is installed with orders to begin cutting costs, or until a new CEO who is not a believer takes over.

MEANWHILE, DOWN IN THE TRENCHES

The story, however, does not end here, for, as we have said earlier, due to the CEO's reluctance to stifle enthusiasm, things have been happening at the unit level. The quality department has made another common mistake. It has tried to organize the entire corporation at once instead of developing model sites in the various divisions and using them as training grounds. Middle-level managers have been trained during the seminars and then sent back to their units to lead the effort there with support from corporate quality.

Yet in most instances, this hasn't actually happened. Even if those trained at the seminars have miraculously learned all they need to know, the chance of accomplishing anything once they return to their units is slim. Most are already overloaded with operating responsibilities and don't have the time. Those who do must first deal with the doubts of peers. Also, because the small corporate quality department staff has so much territory to cover, the amount of support that it can offer each facility is minimal.

Several units have decided to strike out on their own. A number of ambitious facility and department heads, with a feel for what is required and a smaller, less complex, more unified operation to mold, has read the right books and picked good consultants, putting at least a partially successful model into place. There has been a noticeable improvement in both morale and bottom line.

Once these positive results have started to occur, the managers responsible for them have naturally wanted to spread the word. Yet despite the presentations, video tapes, and units' continually improving performance and bottom line, the desired response has not materialized. The head of quality has generally avoided the involved sites and, in some cases, has actually tried to play down their successes. At the same time, due to the fiercely competitive corporate culture, other upper-level managers and directors have shown little real interest. Instead, they have persisted in working on their own personalized models based on their own readings, their own seminars, and their own consultants.

What has evolved, then, at the facility or department level, is a diverse scattering of partially successful efforts to encourage commitment, cooperation, and integration, which, in effect, are committed mainly to their own success, do not cooperate, and are not integrated.

This result is obviously not the one that the CEO had hoped for, causing him or her to wonder if the company can afford to keep pouring time and money into an effort that promises such great things but that, in actuality, continues to deliver relatively little in terms of meaningful bottom-line and quality-of-working-life improvements.

FINAL DETAILS

Several final points concerning the traditional organization learning curve in quality improvement efforts should be covered. One has to do with the misconception that training is the most important phase of any QIP. A second has to do with the nature of reward systems developed as part of such efforts. A third has to do with the generation of ways to measure the success of QIPs.

Training is not the most important phase. Tom Peters is a bonafide quality guru. When he speaks of our nation's need to focus on quality, he is excellent. Yet one assertion of his that may be considered incomplete is that in order to improve quality companies need to train, train, train, train, train, and then to retrain. While in government it is said that if you want nothing to happen you form a committee to study the issue in depth, in quality improvement efforts the same result is achieved by mounting a never-ending cycle of training.

This is not to suggest that training is unimportant. It is not only important but requisite on both the technical and management skills sides. What Mr. Peters leaves out is that employees must first understand the need for and the value of the involved training if it is to produce the desired results. Until this necessary level of understanding is reached, a great deal of what is said will, unfortunately, fall on uncomprehending or uninterested ears.

If a most important phase must be chosen, it would be the team building phase—the putting into place of a team network that facilitates communicating with and gaining input from employees on all levels. A growing number of people agrees with this chapter's key assertion that commitment must be the top priority of any successful quality improvement effort.

An organization gains commitment by respecting employees—showing that it wants their input, that it is eager to listen to and implement their ideas when they make sense. Teams have proven the best vehicle for the generation and implementation of such input and ideas. Teams, then, are also the best vehicle for generating the necessary level of commitment. This point will be expounded on in later chapters.

Corporations also earn employee commitment by showing a willingness to share the financial rewards gained from extra effort. Many companies have developed elaborate non-bottom-line-based recognition and award programs. These suffice in the short term to keep process momentum going but not in the long term. This point will also be elaborated on later in the book.

Finally, many companies spend a great deal of time at the beginning of their effort developing quantitative techniques for measuring success. Most of these techniques fail to produce reliable results. For one thing, the amounts involved are difficult, if not impossible, to measure accurately. How, for example, do you put a dollar value on improved communication between manufacturing and marketing, or between engineering and maintenance? At the same time, project leaders will be tempted to exaggerate if money or numbers become the measure of their achievement. They will also begin to compete, although competition within and between functions is something that the process tries to limit or eliminate completely.

Perhaps more important is the fact that even if they were reliable, most of these techniques fail to produce meaningful results. Saving $100,000 here or $200,000 there by trying something new doesn't matter if other parts of the organization are not keeping pace. What QIPs must strive for is a well-integrated effort that eventually changes the nature of the whole organization. The two most realistic and comprehensive measures of such a holistic transformation are improvement in the bottom line on the quantitative side and improvement in employee morale on the qualitative side.

In summary, then, the problems encountered in quality improvement efforts can usually be traced to top-level management's failure to understand the complexity of such an undertaking. As a result of this failure, the newly appointed head of quality is frequently put into an impossible position. That person is required to lead an effort to reeducate an entire work force, to reorient both management systems and the organization's attitude toward technology after learning in several months what should take at least a year. Sometimes the learning must take place in his or her spare time. To make matters worse, the new quality head must do all this while contending with efforts mounted by ambitious in-house competitors.

Quality improvement is a relatively new concept in our corporate world. We have moved rapidly in the right direction, but we have taken shortcuts that have frustrated us. Perhaps now is the time to regroup. One way of doing this is to begin thinking systemically about quality improvement.

The first step has been to identify the pieces that must at least be understood before we can successfully begin. The next step, then, is to develop an idealized, generic model that gives us a clear idea of the whole that we are shooting for when we begin implementation. It must be specific enough to allow us to identify action steps. At the same time, however, it must be general enough so that any type of organization can apply it effectively. We do not want to open ourselves to the criticism made earlier of consulting firms that try to force organizational QIPs into a predetermined format that is inappropriate.

The presentation and explanation of a generic, systemic quality improvement process model will be our objective in Chapter 2.

The Five Phases of a Systemic Quality Improvement Process

TALKING IT UP

Systemic quality improvement processes (QIPs) must include five over-lapping integrated phases. They are familiarization, vehicle emplacement, training, implementation of measurement techniques, and long-range or strategic planning.

During the familiarization phase, which should always come first, upper-level management, quality department staff members, and consultants explain to the entire work force the need for improved quality. They usually begin this process at the top of the organization, working their way down gradually to the hourly ranks. They discuss the fact that after World War II when the United States had little competition, quality was not a major concern. But now that European and Asian nations have caught up technologically and are cutting into our share of the world market, quality has become the decisive battleground.

They help employees realize that a successful quality improvement process is just that. Rather than a project or an exercise with an end, it is an ongoing process that eventually causes the corporate culture to change, to become more participative and better integrated.

They explain the difference between quality control, which basically checks for product defects and then tries to discover and eliminate the causes of these defects, and the new, more comprehensive quality thrust that realizes that better product quality results from improvements in the quality of manufacturing processes, management systems, and the work environment as well.

They stress that the ultimate objective of QIPs *must* be to improve the bottom line, that if the corporation fails financially, the rest is meaningless. They point out that while our traditional emphasis on producing increased quantities, frequently at the expense of quality, does not always lead to such an improvement, a continual emphasis on quality that, in the short run, might even necessitate a cutback in production levels, does.

They discuss the fact that improved quality results primarily from a high level of employee commitment and that three things are fundamental to this high level: management emphasis on insuring job security; reasonable levels of pay; and respect for employee work-related ideas and needs.

They discuss the fact that upper-level management cannot dominate or channel the process, at least initially, but must show strong support for it, not only with words but with actions: senior executives must function as a resource to employee improvement efforts; upper-level management must constantly encourage and applaud these efforts; and, most important, the CEO must set the example by more fully utilizing the talents of his or her *own* direct reports in the formulation of corporate and department policy.

They talk about the need to involve unions in such efforts, with local representatives being encouraged to play an active role as facilitators, resources, and cheerleaders. A properly run QIP can do nothing but improve the situation of employees. Progressive union leaders understand this and actively support such efforts. Those who resist do so for three reasons:

1. They have experienced such poor relations with management that they oppose any sort of collaboration. They are afraid the effort is a ploy and that, once the union's power is broken, management will revert to its old ways and take unfair advantage of employees.
2. They don't believe that employees are capable of representing themselves adequately in labor-management negotiations.
3. They are afraid of losing their leadership positions as the process draws labor and management closer together.

QIPs have many of the same basic objectives as unions, though a QIP's approach may be different. By different I mean that while many union leaders—especially in the United States—continue to think in win-lose terms, as do many corporate executives, QIPs advocate a win-win approach. Also, QIPs encourage employees to think and speak for themselves. The union leader's role shifts from representing membership directly to supporting, encouraging, and safeguarding members' efforts to voice their own opinions, make their own contributions, and satisfy their own needs.

They explain the team model that has been picked or developed by the head of quality and the group of managers gathered to help shape the effort. They stress the fact that the process will be action rather than training driven. Teams will be formed immediately and will begin working on projects within a week. What employees, especially lower-level ones, need most is a chance to perform, someone to keep them on track, a positive response to their requests, and a rapid initial taste of success to convince them that they indeed have been given the power to create change. Up-front training in problem identification, problem-solving, and group process techniques is usually a waste of time. Employees already know the problems because they live with them. Also, they often have a pretty good idea of excellent solutions and, with proper support, are quick to ferret them out.

At the same time, familiarizers try to make clear that what is about to be attempted will take a long time; while positive changes will occur almost at once, it might take years before the sought-after new culture is finally in place.

They end by making the point that the process will survive only if it proves beneficial to employees and to the company. At this point, the company asks only that people give it a chance. A fairly safe bet would be that every single employee can think of at least one way to improve a product, manufacturing process, management system, or the work environment. The QIP will provide the opportunity to turn these ideas into reality.

In summation, the familiarization phase is self-defining. Its purpose is to offer the "why?" behind a QIP and the "what do we need to put into place to accomplish our objectives?" It is ongoing. Presentations are made continually, at all employee levels, with shifting emphasis depending on the audience and the process stage. Tools used during the familiarization phase can include posters, videos, presentations, stickers, visits to other sites—anything that will help employees: focus on improved quality as a primary workplace objective; better comprehend the power being given them; and better understand the corporation's customized approach.

MISTAKE TIME

Once the familiarization phase is well under way, most corporations make their first serious mistake. Several versions of this mistake are possible. The most common, as we have said, is that they jump from familiarization directly to training rather than to team building. One of the major reasons that so many QIPs lose themselves so quickly in training is that most quality consultants and members of QIP departments attempting to deal with the "socio" or human side of the equation versus the "technical" side have backgrounds in organization behavior, organization development, or psychology. Their skills lie primarily in training, in working directly with individuals' problems and group processes. The systems approach focuses instead on organization systems. It asserts that if employees can improve these systems, most work-related employee problems will vanish without individual counselling.

In addition to conceptual weaknesses, there are also serious process-related weaknesses in QIPs that stress the training phase and neglect others, especially the vehicle emplacement phase. For one thing, such efforts are usually top-down. Professional trainers, following the lead of those who organized the familiarization phase, begin by training upper- and middle-level managers, who, in turn, are supposed to train lower-level managers and hourly workers with the support of the professionals. But there is a critical difference between the familiarization phase and the training phase. While the up-front portion of the former can be presented to large audiences and completed in several weeks, the latter, when dealing with a company of any size, ultimately involves running several thousand students through well-organized two- to three-day sessions. Such an effort is extremely drawn out so that by the time that everyone is trained, many of the earlier students have lost their enthusiasm, their workshop notebooks, or both.

At the same time, such training is rarely if ever adequate. Learning a technique in the classroom, even practicing it there, never gives students all the answers or prepares them fully for the real-life situation. A tremendous amount of support, therefore, is necessary when those initially trained begin passing down their new knowledge and skills to lower-level managers and hourly workers. Such support, however, is rarely available. The corporate quality staff and consultants can visit just so many work sites during the year and can answer just so many phone calls.

Also, many middle managers see QIPs as an attempt to get rid of their jobs. They've heard about too many layers of management and about the push to get hourly workers to make more work-related decisions so that some of these layers can be eliminated. Giving middle-level managers the responsibility of passing on problem-solving and decision-making skills is, in many cases, like asking the last werewolf to teach the pretty lady how to shoot silver bullets. It doesn't make sense. Inexperienced or emotional supervisors create a fuss or refuse openly to cooperate. The old-timers go through the motions but then make sure that nothing happens.

Finally, when a comprehensive training effort is mounted before the vehicle is put into place, employees receive little or no chance to contribute to the design of the package. What they get, therefore, is frequently not what they need. As a result, the employees must either go without due to their reticence to complain when management is so enthusiastic, or they must be retrained at some later date.

VERSION TWO

The second version of the mistake made following the familiarization phase is that the corporation decides to jump directly to the introduction of statistical measurement techniques (SQC and SPC). Again, the belief is that the involved education effort will provide the apparatus for generating employee commitment. It will not. What many of us have done is to misinterpret the producers of Edward Deming's success in Japan. One of the major differences between the traditional Japanese and U.S. work forces is that with the former, commitment to the good of the organization as a whole is a given. It is a cultural characteristic. The problem that Deming faced, therefore, was not to foster but rather to effectively channel an already existing sense of commitment and teamwork. In this situation, SQC was a useful tool in the right place at the right time.

Due to the traditional adversarial relationship between labor and management in the U.S. work force, however, we must begin at the beginning. The first step must be to generate the necessary level of commitment to improved quality. Without it, the introduction of measurement techniques will be seen, in its best light, as having nothing to do with the betterment of the worker's situation. In its worst, it will be seen as a threat to job security and something that must be blocked.

VERSION THREE

The third version of the mistake is that a poorly thought out, poorly integrated, and poorly facilitated aggregate of teams or quality circles is put into place. These teams produce few results that are beneficial in the long run, consume an inappropriate amount of time, and end up frustrating everyone involved. This failure gives the quality effort a bad name and makes it difficult to reenergize the process once the necessary lessons have been learned.

Vehicle emplacement must follow the familiarization phase and must be done correctly. The team network is the most important part of the puzzle for the following reasons:

1. The teams provide a visible structure for the entire process. They form a focused framework that supports the ongoing familiarization, training, measurement technique introduction, and strategic planning phases.

2. QIPs ultimately live or die, as we have said, according to the bottom-line improvements that they produce. If the teams in the network are properly organized, each will begin working on and completing projects two to four weeks after it is formed. The process will soon produce measurable financial returns, thus relieving upper-level management's anxiety about the bottom-line value of the exercise.

3. Again, commitment from employees on all levels is the most necessary ingredient to a successful QIP, and team activities, more than anything else, help generate that commitment.

Teams must be formed in all parts and on all levels of the organization. Teams of hourly workers should be formed first. They should be formed by function, breaking down the operation, to start with, into its smallest complete parts. In order to generate the desired level of commitment, these hourly teams should initially include no managers. This allows members to gain process ownership. It keeps team sessions from turning into "business as usual," with management taking the lead and defining priorities. Eventually, after team members understand the process and have completed several projects, they may invite one or two popular first-line managers to join. The decision on each, however, must be unanimous.

At the same time, managers need their own teams so that they can work on improvements that they think important. Management teams can be formed one per division, including all levels of management in that division; or by level, including all managers on that level across the organization; or by level by division, if the organization is large enough. Management teams generally address larger issues than hourly teams. While an hourly team is worried about accessing specific information on their unit terminals, for example, a management team might want to reorganize the entire information network for that division. Hourly team projects are frequently related to larger-scale management team projects and must eventually be integrated.

Teams should meet according to a set schedule. They must be led through an initial exercise to help them identify and prioritize what they want to work on. Their members must communicate team activities to those they represent and get their input. Hourly teams must be protected from managers who remain opposed to and attempt to frustrate their efforts. Team activities must be fully integrated on all levels. The team effort must have a set of ground rules that are well thought out, and understood and agreed to by everyone.

Finally, team building efforts should start at the shipping dock or the sales counter and move from there backward through the product development steps. This is important for several reasons. First, if this approach is used, customers are more likely to benefit from early improvements. Second, in terms of identifying functional boundaries, most of the problems first identified by teams concern their relationship with the previous rather than the following production function. For example, the packaging unit is certainly more concerned with what it receives from the manufacturing unit than with what it sends on to shipping. The idea is to have the team building phase flow in the same direction as team interests and activities.

TRAINING AS A PARTICIPATIVE CHALLENGE

The training phase starts soon after the first teams are in place and follows the team building phase through the organization. It "follows" because initial facilitator training is done on the job and because team members identify a large number of their own training needs.

Teams have facilitators and not leaders. The facilitator's job is basically to make sure that the ground rules are obeyed, to help keep meetings on track, to function as a resource or resource generator, and to help coordinate team activities with those of the other teams in the network. The facilitator cannot be any team member's boss. Employees must realize through the team process that they can and should begin thinking for themselves, that the company can no longer afford for them to wait to be told what to do. This change in workplace attitude is nearly impossible if a boss is given the same position of control in the team meeting that he or she has on the office or shop floor.

The facilitator can be either an hourly person or a manager but should be from another part of the operation so that personal opinions about the best solution to the problem being worked on do not confuse his or her role. The facilitator, as we have said, is initially trained on the job. After a brief familiarization session concerning the team building process, each facilitator sits in on team meetings led by a consultant or an experienced facilitator. Eventually, the new facilitator is given the lead, with the consultant observing and supporting. Once several facilitators have been trained in this manner and begin communicating, they help to identify other training needs, set up their own training sessions, and assist each other with insights.

Team members also receive almost no initial training. They are taught a very simple problem-solving technique, mainly by applying it to the first actual improvement on which they decide to work. Further training needs are identified, at least in part by the team itself. A majority of them are technical rather than related to group process. These needs fall roughly into four categories:

1. Additional job training for new employees who were not adequately trained when their responsibilities were first assigned.
2. Cross-training once employees have become proficient in their own areas of expertise.
3. More training on new equipment now that employees have become familiar enough with it to identify what their weaknesses are.
4. Training concerning the organization-wide production process so that employees can better understand how they fit into it.

THE INTRODUCTION OF MEASUREMENT TECHNIQUES

In a production unit of a thousand or so, educating quality department staff to the nuances of the five-phase process, familiarizing everyone, creating and integrating the necessary network of teams, forming and integrating the necessary network of facilitators, and providing all the critical and requested training will probably take more than a year. By the end of this period, however, even though all the teams might not yet be operational, a critical mass should have materialized or be well on its way to materializing.

In a QIP, the concept of "critical mass" relates to the point at which enough people understand and believe in the value of the process that it can't be stopped except by executive edict. It refers to the time when the process takes on a life of its own. Workers and managers rather than consultants now conduct the ongoing familiarization effort. Trained in-house staff take the new teams through their initial problem identification and prioritization exercise. Training needs have been well defined and met. The teams have generated several hundred useful improvements and have been continually applauded for their efforts by top-level management.

Also by this time, many teams have solved all the simple problems affecting their productivity and are realizing that additional improvements will be more difficult. They are beginning to understand the complexity of the operation. It is at this point, then, that measurement techniques can be effectively introduced as a potential aid to their continuing efforts.

The stage is set. The trick, however, is to give the teams ownership, to let *them* decide that what is being offered is a good idea and should be spread throughout the operation. The basic techniques involved—histograms, run charts, control charts, flow charts, pareto, the fishbone, and scatter charts—are not that difficult to teach or to use. The hard part traditionally has been to get employees to *want* to use them.

There are three possible approaches. The first is coercion: learn how to use these or start looking for another job. However, when employees are forced to implement something they don't understand the need for, they tend to make a lot of mistakes.

The second approach is to educate workers to the value of measurement techniques. Conscientious and ambitious employees will listen and will make a sincere effort to implement what they have learned. Those just putting in their hours, however, will see the additional time and effort requirement as another unwelcome imposition and will take shortcuts.

The third approach is to encourage the employees themselves to discover the value of the techniques. Chances for successful implementation increase greatly when team members begin saying things like, "We need to understand the entire pattern of paper flow in this office before we can successfully resolve bottlenecks," or "The only way we're going to find out what's wrong with this machine is to keep an accurate record of variations in run quality." When this last approach is taken, managers and trainers are no longer totally responsible for convincing workers of the techniques' value. Also, rather than managers having to make sure that everyone enters their data points correctly, the employees themselves willingly accept this responsibility. They keep tabs on, encourage, and assist each other because *they* have ownership.

The third scenario is obviously superior, but how do we achieve it? We do so primarily by developing a strong sense of employee commitment to improved quality in products, manufacturing processes, management systems, and the work environment. But how do we engender this required commitment? The answer is that we foster it through the familiarization, vehicle emplacement, and training phases that precede the introduction of measurement techniques.

STRATEGIC PLANNING REBORN

In order for QIP organizers, familiarizers, team facilitators, trainers, and team members to succeed, they must have a framework built on clearly defined organization objectives into which to fit their integrated efforts. This framework, or overview, traditionally has been created through the annual strategic planning exercise. Recently, however, strategic planning has fallen on hard times. It is no longer considered a critical function in many corporations. The future of such organizations is now being decided by the president or CEO and a few confidantes, their decisions based on a mix of financial considerations, their own observations, and gut instinct.

The reason for the recent disenchantment with strategic planning is twofold. First, our much maligned short-term orientation makes the ability to react quickly to shifting environmental circumstances more important than the ability to generate a long-term plan. Second, even if our orientation were long term, strategic planning, as it has been practiced during the seventies and eighties, does not work.

According to Russell Ackoff's article "The Corporate Rain Dance," which appeared in the Winter 1977 issue of *The Wharton Magazine*, strategic planning, during this period, was carried out strictly in either a "bottom-up" or "top-down" fashion. In the bottom-up approach, word was sent out annually for low-level unit heads to put together and prioritize their budget requests, then to submit these requests to their superiors, who were to do the same thing, and so on until final lists reached the top for scrutiny and further deletions.

The weaknesses of this approach were many. First, the budget estimates were never accurate. Management expected requests to be inflated and automatically cut the amount allowed. In order to get what they actually needed, therefore, departments doubled or tripled their projected requirements. Second, decisions made at the various levels concerning the lists coming in from the next lowest echelon were frequently influenced by corporate politics or were based on insufficient information. Third, very little true integration of departmental priority lists occurred, as units were forced by the process to compete for resources.

The top-down approach began with the formation of a strategic planning department. This department was separate from the rest of the company and reported directly to the CEO. Its role was to do ongoing research and to develop models and projections concerning technology, the market, the competition, raw materials, capital, the political situation, and so on. It was to consolidate this information into recommendations from which the CEO could devise a set of overall long-term corporate objectives. These objectives would then be passed down so that each department and level could define the changes and activities in its area necessary to meet them.

The problems with the top-down approach were also many. To begin with, due to the continually increasing number of relevant variables in the organization's environment, it was impossible to identify all of the important ones in a model. Even if one did succeed in this herculean task, however, due to the increasing amount of turbulence in the relationships between the involved variables, suppositions drawn that were correct one day might not be correct the next day, or the next week, or the next month. By then corporate and departmental objectives had been defined and units had begun planning so that word had to be sent down to modify. Yet while the necessary adjustments were being made, a second critical variable began shifting, or was threatening to shift, and so on.

Corporate objectives defined in this top-down manner also frequently failed to take into account the situation at lower levels. Impossible demands were made that eventually had to be modified, thus affecting the organization's ability to meet its original objectives. Finally, the necessary degree of integration between departmental efforts rarely occurred.

Strategic planning is important, not only to quality improvement but to the long-term health of any organization. Asian and European firms do it effectively and have used the results to increase their share of world markets. The problem, therefore, is not that strategic planning does not work but that the paradigms that we have been using in the United States are not right for our situation.

In order to be more successful, we need an approach that helps replace or combine our short-term orientation with a long-term one; discourages in-house competition for resources; helps generate consensus on priorities; encourages the necessary integration; effectively reads and reacts to the organization's increasingly turbulent environment; and does not impose unrealistic demands on those required to translate corporate objectives, as defined, into reality.

The interactive planning paradigm developed by Ackoff and described in his book *Creating the Corporate Future* meets all of the above criteria. It also enjoys a comfortable fit with and is fueled by the other four phases of a comprehensive QIP. Interactive planning has several key characteristics. First, it is *participative*. All employees are expected to contribute to and learn from the process. This helps foster the necessary consensus and integration. Also, it helps avoid surprises and unreasonable demands, enlists the aid of the entire workforce in spotting shifts in key variables, and greatly enriches the quality of input.

An obvious objection to such extensive participation is that it draws out the planning process. The time factor, however, becomes irrelevant when we learn that the second critical characteristic of interactive planning is its *continuous* nature. When an organization chooses this paradigm, planning is no longer seen as a time-consuming annual exercise. Rather, it becomes part of the normal daily or weekly routine. This characteristic allows the plan to evolve and to improve as shifts in key environmental variables occur. Short-term needs also can now be taken into account but are framed in terms of realistic long-term objectives.

The third key characteristic of interactive planning is that it is *holistic*, addressing every part and level of the organization simultaneously and making sure that what is generated is well integrated.

Interactive planning, like comprehensive quality improvement efforts, has five overlapping stages. These are formulation of the mess; ends planning; means planning; resource planning; and implementation and control.

Formulation of the Mess—A "mess" is defined by Ackoff in "The Corporate Rain Dance" as a system of problems. During this stage the future of an organization if no changes are made and if the environment remains stable is charted. The stage includes a comprehensive series of systems analyses covering both the organization's internal operations and its environment, as well as traditional reference projections. It synthesizes all of the above into a reference scenario that more graphically and creatively shows employees where they are now and the types of changes necessary if the organization wants to improve on or even to maintain its current level of success.

While some of the above exercises, such as the reference projections, need to be conducted by professionals such as those found in the traditional "top-down" planning department, others can be contributed to by QIP teams.

Ends Planning—During this stage participants define an "ideal." They are told that their company, mill, or department has been destroyed and that they are responsible for totally rebuilding it. The charge, however, is to design what *ought* to be ideally, rather than simply to improve on what originally existed. The only three stipulations to this exercise are that the systems designed must be technologically feasible, financially reasonable, and capable of adapting to future environmental change.

Everyone is involved. Executives begin with the organization as a whole, idealizing its overall mission, objectives, and goals. Supervisors begin with management systems. Hourly workers begin with their manufacturing processes and work environment. As the designs are completed, they are integrated with those of bordering units and reworked in terms of this broadened perspective.

Once completed, the final, comprehensive idealization gives the company an agreed upon target to aim for so that the limited number of changes a yearly budget will allow makes sense as part of a long-term, well-integrated whole. At the same time, the exercise result continues to evolve and improve.

Again, the organization-wide team network provides a perfect vehicle for an idealization exercise. The teams in a QIP progress naturally from problem solving to design challenges, from quick fixes such as the demarkation of pedestrian lanes in a warehouse to reorganizing the warehouse so that there is less traffic overall. When teams begin addressing design challenges, they should be taught the idealization technique, so that this stage of interactive planning is already occurring piecemeal throughout the facility.

Means Planning—During this stage projects that will help move the organization from its current "mess" toward the ideal are defined and prioritized. The QIP teams can play a key role in both definition and prioritization once overall organization objectives have been identified.

Resource Planning—The teams can contribute heavily to both the identification of available resources and allocation decisions.

Implementation and Control—The teams can assist in carrying out action steps. They can also generate the information necessary for proper control and function as a channel for the upward and downward flow of this information.

Concerning the introduction of strategic planning, which is the fifth phase of a comprehensive QIP, timing is critical. As mentioned earlier, hourly and supervisory teams *must* be allowed to gain the necessary degree of process and team project ownership before upper-level management asks them for help or otherwise directly orients their efforts. Planners must wait at least until a critical mass has developed to begin using the quality process vehicle to achieve their own ends. They can ask individual employees, shifts, or departments for assistance, they can form task forces, but they cannot use the QIP teams.

The other side of the coin is that the CEO or unit manager, and his or her direct reports, should start their own idealization exercise as soon as possible. The objectives defined at this level will indirectly impact every other team's perspective and activities by providing the previously mentioned organization-wide framework.

ALL OR NOTHING

All systemic and successful QIPs must include the five phases discussed in this chapter. None of these phases can provide the desired results without the support of the others. Familiarization is of little value without a change vehicle, training, and a framework of long-range organization objectives. Teams cannot function effectively without proper familiarization, relevant training, and long-range objectives. Training is largely a waste of time without a change vehicle and a framework of objectives. Measurement tools are all but useless by themselves. Finally, a strategic plan has no value unless employees understand it, are committed to it, and possess the knowledge and skills necessary to implement it.

While all five phases are important, vehicle emplacement, or team building, is the most critical. Team building is also the most difficult phase to introduce. A majority of team building efforts in the United States have failed. They have done so mainly because those responsible have not understood the systemic nature of the beast that they were trying to tame and have left out critical pieces, or have been unable to link the pieces together properly.

Chapter 3, then, will discuss a systemic approach to team building.

Ground Rules—
Quality Improvement Process Glue

TEAM BUILDING AS A TRAUMATIC EXPERIENCE

A majority of corporate attempts in this country to put an effective network of participative teams or quality circles into place has not produced the desired results. What we have learned from this experience is that the team building effort, as part of a systemic quality improvement process, is not as simple as it might first appear. Reasons for the lack of success in such efforts include the following:

—Team members miss meetings due to production crises and other demands on their time and have difficulty getting involved.

—Management sees the team network as a vehicle for accomplishing its own objectives and begins dictating team projects or taking over team meetings.

—Teams eventually bury themselves, becoming involved in so many projects at once that nothing gets finished and members lose interest.

—Teams take on projects that are too difficult, slow moving, and long term so that members again lose interest.

—Team meetings degenerate rapidly into gripe sessions.

—Team members start squabbling, or factions develop with conflict-ing interests.

—Teams function for several weeks or months, then disband, as members are disillusioned by the lack of support for or reaction to their ideas.

—Teams get into trouble with other teams and departments because the changes they make have unexpected, negative consequences on other parts of the operation.

—Actual and suggested changes generated by teams are seen as a threat by supervision and are blocked.

The missing piece that can prevent all of the above is a well-thought-out, well-defined set of ground rules agreed to by everyone from the CEO or facility manager on down. There must also be a mechanism built into the ground rules that insures that they will be obeyed by everyone affected by or capable of affecting the process. Such ground rules are the glue that holds the team building phase of a QIP together; but because the team network can be used as the vehicle to continue the familiarization phase, for both definition and implementation of necessary technical and man-agement skills training, for the implementation of measurement tech-niques, and for the strategic planning effort, the glue that holds the team network together is actually foundational to the entire comprehensive effort and must contain the right mixture of ingredients.

The main purpose of this chapter, then, is to present the ground rules developed in our search for a systemic whole.

GROUND RULES

1. Teams must meet, at least initially, on a regular basis, and members must attend.

Initially, quality team meetings usually are of low priority when super-visors are scheduling the time of their hourly workers. Telling supervisors that the process will produce improvements is not sufficient. They have to be shown. Several meetings will pass before the teams start generating notable results. Therefore, supervisors must be forced to arrange coverage for process participants and, unless a true crisis occurs, to release them for the hour to hour and a half required weekly.

This ground rule insures that team members get a chance to learn the value of the process before deciding whether or not to remain involved.

When the first teams are brought up, asking for volunteers frequently does not work. No matter how thorough the initial familiarization session has been, hourly workers see the meetings mainly as an additional responsibility, especially if they must attend during nonworking hours. Potential benefits of the process are suspect. Most employees have long since given up hope of seriously impacting the operation with their ideas.

Supervisors should identify the employees that they think most capable of contributing something of value, then make the initial four meetings mandatory for these people. After this introductory period, team members should be able to replace themselves if they remain unconvinced. Eventually, efforts should be made to rotate team membership so that as many employees as possible have the opportunity to experience this new way of dealing with problematic issues and of making contributions, and so that original team members do not burn out.

> *2. Teams must find substitutes for members who leave them and for members who are on vacation, sick leave, or absent for any other reason.*

Another way of involving more employees is to require team members with legitimate reasons for missing a meeting to send a substitute. This requirement also encourages team members to keep the coworkers that they represent informed of team activities. If they don't, it will be much more difficult to find a substitute when needed. In some instances, substitutes become so involved that the team designates them as regular alternates. In others, it is necessary to expand the team to include employees who want very much to participate on a full-time basis.

> *3. Teams must be allowed to identify the projects they want to work on themselves.*

After making sure that compensation is adequate and demonstrating concern for job security, the most effective way for management to foster the requisite level of commitment is by showing employees an appropriate amount of respect for their expertise, ideas, and personal needs. This can be done by giving teams the right to choose the projects that they want to work on.

When teams are given this right, some supervisors fear that time will be wasted on relatively superficial improvements. Sometimes it is. Supervisors learn, however, often to their surprise, that hourly workers have a good understanding both of the problems in their work areas and of their relative importance. Another value of allowing teams to identify the projects that they wish to work on concerns ownership. Most corporate heads agree that employees work harder on improvements for which the employees themselves have defined the need, and that they are more eager to see such projects through to a satisfactory conclusion.

> *4. All team members are equal. Any supervisor involved, for example, must "remove his or her hat" during meetings.*

On the shop or office floor, there are bosses and workers, but during the weekly team session anyone who attends either as a team member or a guest must "take off his or her hat." The immediate suspicion is that supervisors will have trouble doing so. In some cases this is true. Some supervisors simply do not want their workers to get involved in what they consider to be management decisions, no matter how low level, and are sure that any improvement that the work force might suggest will be poorly thought out, too expensive, or both.

After some initial uneasiness, most supervisors, however, realize two things. The first is that meetings provide one of the few real opportunities that they have to hear what the workers think and to talk with them informally. The second is that the problem-solving and design exercises, besides producing useful results in most cases, are also a tremendous learning vehicle for team members. Rather than trying to take over, therefore, most supervisors are quite happy to function as a resource to team efforts.

> *5. Teams must prioritize their problem list and work on correcting the problems one at a time until an acceptable stage of progress is reached on each. They should be encouraged to start with the simplest.*

One of the major concerns, especially with teams composed of hourly workers, is keeping members focused. They tend to jump from one problem to another, defining a few action steps for each, but completing very little, as new projects are continually introduced and pieces of the old ones are lost. Once members have compiled the initial list of problems and improvements that they want to address, they should be instructed to pick one project and work on it until all action steps possible at that point have been defined and assigned. Only then can a second project be chosen and work started.

Team facilitators should encourage members to begin with relatively easy projects. The objective is to produce some quick positive results so that team members realize that they can indeed have an impact and so that supervisors realize that the teams are capable of effectively addressing lower-level, day-to-day, "nuts-and-bolts" issues, releasing the supervisors to focus on the larger, more systemic challenges that they had been wanting to address for months, even years.

> 6. *Team members are not allowed to complain about a situation unless they are able to suggest a reasonable way to improve it.*

No job is perfect. Once team members realize that they really do control the weekly sessions, there is a tendency to use them to vent frustrations against supervisors, other shifts, the benefits department, contractors, consultants, and so on. An hour to an hour and a half per week is not much time, and frequently, after the first six months or so, teams start meeting every other week. Griping can consume entire sessions, producing nothing positive except the temporary relief of the gripee's frustration.

Therefore, meetings must be organized to utilize time effectively. The following agenda is suggested:

1. Review previously defined action steps of ongoing projects,
2. Record achievements,
3. Continue problem-solving effort with ongoing projects,
4. Define further action steps for ongoing projects,
5. Identify new priority projects to be worked on, when appropriate,
6. Identify new projects to be added to the list.

This is not to say that all griping is automatically eliminated from the sessions. Especially during early, formative meetings, it is necessary to allow members to ramble some. Gradually, however, the facilitator must become sterner. Most team members will appreciate and support this ground rule. The griping is nothing new. But the opportunity to make positive change is, and they'll want to take advantage of it.

> 7. *All team decisions will be reached through consensus.*

The long-range objective of any QIP is to develop an integrated system of operations that employees on all levels understand and support. The foundation from which this system grows is the team network. Understanding of and support for the necessary changes in products, manufacturing processes, management systems, and work environment begin here and must be based on consensus.

When consensus cannot be reached on team logistical issues such as which operational problem to work on first, the reason is frequently that too many different areas of interest have been combined on one team. When two solutions to the same operational problem continue to be supported, the best way to solve the dispute and reach consensus is to get input from additional knowledgeable stakeholders.

   8. *Teams have access to all company personnel to meet their information needs.*

The team process is both a learning and a change exercise. Its strength, in terms of the former, is that team members themselves identify their learning needs. The willingness of an organization to make available the requested informational resources shows its continuing support for and realization of the value of the team process, and its understanding that employees can make a valuable contribution if given access to the information they think important.

While access to all in-house personnel must be guaranteed, this ground rule should also apply to suppliers, customers, contractors, and other outside stakeholders whenever possible.

The president or facility manager is a favorite invitee to early team meetings. Members are curious to see if he or she will actually appear. Most managers see this series of half-hour sessions as worthwhile expenditures of their time. After the initial visit, however, it must be explained to team members that project-related information usually can be supplied by someone other than the president or facility manager and that teams should work their way up in terms of resources rather than always starting at the top.

   9. *Improvements/projects that might influence other parts of the operation must be agreed to by anyone else affected. Such stakeholders must also have a chance to contribute before implementation occurs.*

A shift, department, or office supervisor decides that there must be a better way of completing a task. He or she asks a few questions, then figures out and institutes the better way. Workers learn about the change after the fact and don't have the nerve to tell the supervisor that he or she has forgotten something important and, in the long run, has made the situation worse rather than better. A week or two later, other shifts, departments, or offices, which the supervisor claims to have notified prior to the change, begin calling to say that they knew nothing about it and to ask if "Joe realizes how badly he's screwed us up over here?"

All of us are familiar with the above scenario. In order to avoid it, teams are required when developing a solution or designing an innovation to explain it to anyone who will be affected by it or who will help with implementation so that these stakeholders can challenge it or contribute from their own perspective. This process must lead to an eventual consensus and must be completed before implementation steps are outlined. A side benefit of such negotiations is that the involved stakeholder groups learn about other operations and about the nature of their relationships with each other.

This ground rule is the one most frequently broken. Once teams realize that they *truly* have been given the power to create change, they jealously guard projects, not wanting outsiders to interfere or cause delays. It is the facilitator's responsibility, at this point, to force members to identify all stakeholders and get their input. If the team has begun identifying or implementing action steps without doing so, the facilitator must make it back step and fill the requirement.

After completing several successful projects, participants understand that they do not lose but gain by obeying this ground rule. Their results are better, enjoy more universal support, and are more loudly applauded.

10. All team minutes are confidential unless released by the team.

Minutes are kept to list, prioritize, and track the progress of all projects. They help team members and other stakeholders achieve the same understanding of what is concluded in each meeting.

Another means of giving teams an enhanced sense of control is by allowing members to decide if, when, and to whom they wish to release their notes. Once they start identifying and getting input from project stakeholders, they quickly realize the need to and the value of letting as many people as possible know what they are working on. Therefore, after several weeks, teams are usually eager to disseminate session notes, especially to upper-level managers as a way of opening a channel of direct communication to them.

11. Team-suggested improvements must be justified by a cost-benefit analysis when possible or by a quality-of-working-life rationale when not.

Requiring teams to justify projects is important for several reasons. First, it forces them to discover whether the proposed change is economically viable or not. It is a lot easier to say, "We need a new computer because this one is old and too slow," than it is to prove that the cost of a new computer will be offset in a reasonable period of time by savings and increased productivity. Second, it forces them to think improvements through more thoroughly.

In some instances, it is difficult to define quantitatively the benefits of a project. An example would be improving a bathroom that has no heat, a dirty floor, no lock on the door, and graffiti all over the walls. It is a well-established fact, however, that the workplace environment affects employee productivity. Thus, when teams list bathrooms, air quality, lack of access to food machines, too much human traffic moving through their area, leaking roofs, or cold drafts as a priority, wise supervisors listen to and support improvement efforts. The cost of such projects is usually small, while the nonquantifiable payback is great in terms of both improved department morale and a highly visible display of team success.

12. *Response to team questions/suggestions must be received within one week. The response to suggestions can be "yes, go ahead with it," "no, and this is why" with a reasonable explanation, or "let's talk" with a date set.*

Traditionally, workers with problems or ideas for improvements approach the supervisor individually or in small groups. The supervisor listens sympathetically, if there is time, then agrees and says that the matter will be attended to as soon as possible, or disagrees but doesn't have the time to explain why in detail, promising to continue the conversation later. And that's that, until the idea or problem is brought up again by the worker several days, weeks, or months later, with much the same result. The supervisor is not uninterested. Rather, he or she is overloaded, with ideas and problems pouring in continually from all directions to be dealt with during time not consumed by normal operational duties.

One of the values of the team problem-solving and design approach is that it consolidates a majority of these ideas and problems into one list and prioritizes them through consensus, so that rather than 20 different employees with 20 different concerns, the supervisor must respond only to one group representing the whole and seeking help with one, two, or three projects at most. Another value is that team members no longer see the supervisor as a lap into which problems and ideas are dumped for resolution and implementation but as a resource in their efforts to manage projects themselves.

The flip side of the coin is that while the pressure of numbers has decreased greatly, the pressure to respond has grown. This ground rule forces supervisors to take the time to think the issue through and to develop a useful response. If the supervisor can't get back to the team within one week, it forces him or her to explain why and to set the earliest possible date for a meeting with members.

13. *When a ground rule is violated, the team facilitator will meet with the violator for resolution. If the problem is not overcome, the facilitator will report the violation to the head facilitator who coordinates the facilitator network. If the head facilitator cannot resolve the issue, he or she will carry it to the lead team, which is composed of the company president or facility manager and his or her direct reports, to be addressed.*

The requirement of a one-week response time to team questions/suggestions helps expose those supervisors who want to block a QIP and the cultural change to which it leads. A favorite ploy of such people is to support team activities vocally while, at the same time, making sure that nothing gets accomplished. Such supervisors are not generally malicious. Rather, they are conscientious to a fault, firmly believing that if they do not personally control every aspect of the operation, bad things will happen.

The head facilitator's agreement with lead team members that they will, as a last resort, deal directly with such recalcitrance provides the "hammer" that all serious organizational change efforts require. It also helps move upper-level managers into an educational and process advocacy role.

14. *The problem-solving and design teams will pick their own representatives to sit on task forces dealing with issues that cross team boundaries.*

When a problem-solving or design team has to include stakeholders from other teams or departments in a project, there are four ways to get their input. The first and most common is to talk to them during working hours. The second is to send a representative to their meeting. The third, conversely, is to invite them to the originating team's meeting. The fourth, if the project requires a lot of work, is to create a task force to address the issues with each stakeholder group assigning its own representative or representatives.

Task forces can also be formed by the lead team or upper-level management around any project considered important that is not currently being addressed. QIP team members can be drafted to sit on these task forces but not to the exclusion of their team-related activities.

As soon as the involved project is completed, all task forces, no matter what their origin, are dissolved.

SUMMING UP

Ground rules are the glue that binds employee teams and the rest of the organization together, encouraging the generation of thoroughly thought out, well-integrated improvements. They help systematize the quality improvement process and make possible the development of a strong sense of commitment through the realization of beneficial changes in products, manufacturing processes, management systems, and the work environment.

Ground rules, if they are to be truly effective, must eventually be absorbed into the corporate psyche. They cannot be learned in a classroom-type setting. Team members, therefore, are not expected to fully understand their importance or even their meaning when introduced to them during the initial familiarization sessions. The bulk of learning concerning ground rules is done when teams begin struggling with actual problems and improvements. Team members "grow" into them, sometimes even reinventing them as the need for each arises.

PART 2

Trial by Fire

When we focus solely on raising production levels, both overall quality and profits, in the long run, will most likely suffer.

When we focus on improving the quality of our products, our manufacturing processes, our management systems, and our work environment, however, higher production levels and improved profits will, in a majority of cases, be the result.

Higher production levels, then, should be though of as a desired end, along with improved profits, rather than the means. Improved quality is the means.

There's an old saying, "It's easier to talk the talk than to walk the walk." In Part 1 we talked the talk. In Part 2, then, we will describe a successful attempt to walk the walk at two of Core Corporation's primary mills.

The two mills, the Eastern Mill and the Western Mill, presented different challenges. Labor-management relations at the Eastern Mill were relatively good. The work force was stable and experienced. Union locals supported the effort. The mill manager was quick to understand what was being attempted, and gave strong support, both vocally and through actions.

The Western Mill, on the other hand, was in the throes of a strike. A majority of the replacement work force was new and untrained. A new mill manager took over shortly after the team building process began and was too busy with strike-related crises to pay it the attention that the Eastern Mill manager had, though his support was unquestionable.

The fact that the same approach was successfully introduced in these two extremely different sets of circumstances offers at least partial proof of its generic qualities. Learning from the Eastern Mill experience, the Western Mill implemented a version that was a lot richer, but the basics remained the same.

Our "walk" through the Core effort will be presented chronologically so that readers can gain a feel for its evolution. While attempts are made to stick as close as possible to the facts, the viewpoint is obviously that of the Organization Development (OD) Department consultants.

Chapter 13, as we have said, is an idealization, showing what is possible on the corporate level, and then on the community level once a systemic approach and vehicle are in place and have proven themselves on the mill/unit level.

CHAPTER 4

Putting the Pieces Together

THE PROOF IS IN THE PUDDING

During 1985, one of the Core Corporation's primary mills, the Eastern Pulp and Paper Mill, accounted for approximately 20 percent of the corporation's total profits. In so doing, it generated twice as much profit as its nearest competitor. The mill repeated this performance in 1986 and again in 1987.

The mill manager, Rob Dole, was one of the most experienced in the company. During his ten years at the Eastern Mill he had put together a highly regarded team of direct reports. These two facts alone, however, were not enough to account for the sudden and dramatic increase in profits. The mill had invested in new technology. The woodyard, for example, had been reorganized. A new boiler had been built. New computerized control systems had been installed. But again, these investments were not considered the only producers of the upturn. In fact, a number of critical problems remained to be worked out with the new technology before its effects on profits could be truly felt. At the same time, other mills in the system, some with more capacity, had also been reorganizing and computerizing but had not enjoyed the same improvement in their bottom line. What, then, was going on at the Eastern Mill?

In early 1986, a strike began at the Core's largest manufacturing facility, the Western Pulp and Paper Mill. Despite appeals from union officials not to fill the approximately 1,000 hourly openings, applicants, attracted by the relatively high wage levels, quickly did so. A majority of the replacement workers had no experience in paper making. Supervisors and staff people left their offices to conduct on-the-job training and to keep the machines running. Maintenance personnel were sent in from all over the company to make much needed improvements and to help repair the damage done by strikers when they left. Twelve- to 18-hour work days were not uncommon.

The strike dragged on for over a year. Most of the replacement workers lived 50 to 100 miles from the mill. Each day they had to drive through a gauntlet of jeering, cursing pickets to get to the mill gate. When they headed home at shift change, again the pickets were waiting. Morale was low, exhaustion widespread. Several serious industrial accidents occurred.

Less than two years later, this same group of relatively inexperienced hourly workers and old-time supervisors set an all-time production record. Two months after setting it, they broke it. Three months later, they broke it again. Quite a bit of money had been spent to improve the mill's technical systems, more than was spent on any other production facility during this period. Most employees, however, agreed that a major factor in this success story was the change that had occurred in the mill management culture. It was the same change that Rob Dole credited with precipitating the exceptional performance of the Eastern Mill. Its source, in both situations, was the approach to quality improvement discussed in Part 1.

THE RIGHT MIX

The purpose of Part 2, then, is to show how this approach was successfully implemented in two extremely different manufacturing situations. Describing events in their chronological sequence will provide the framework for this section. Emphasis, however, will be on developing a "feel" for what happened. What we are talking about is a cultural change effort, and, as has been pointed out in the literature many times before, cultural change is as much or more so a matter of emotion than it is of intellect. The "feel" for such a process that people experience in their gut becomes equally or more important than the understanding that they achieve in their brains.

Two critical events occurred at Core Corporation during 1983. The first was the kicking off of a quality improvement process. Core followed the traditional route. Senior executives visited companies that had mounted successful processes, including General Electric, Ford, and Westinghouse.

They talked to Deming, Crosby, and Juran. Then they generated corporate goals, a quality policy, and management principles that complemented the goals and the policy.

The leader selected for the effort was a bright, young "star" with an engineering background. The first task that he and his staff undertook was to organize seminars. Approximately half the company's employees were introduced to the new corporate goals, quality policy, and management principles. One quarter of the company's employees were then familiarized with team building skills and statistical quality control techniques. Finally, a head facilitator, chosen from each facility in the company, received several additional days of training.

The new vice-president of the QIP reported directly to the corporate CEO. His staff consisted of four specialists. One was responsible for developing measurement tools. A second was in charge of ongoing development of the corporate approach. The other two were in charge of facilitating and guiding the efforts of the more than 100 manufacturing facilities and support units scattered across North America.

The second event, initially unrelated, was that Don Green, director of the Organization Development (OD) Section of the Human Relations Division, reorganized his staff, bringing in three new people. One was Ed Miller, who had been with Core for 10 years. Ed had started as a cost analyst. He had then worked as the manager of finance at a primary mill, a senior analyst with Strategic Planning for Paper Board and Packaging, and a senior analyst for New Products Development before coming to OD.

Gail Forbes had a background in counselling and a Ph.D. in organization behavior. She had worked previously as a trainer with a major consulting firm and as an internal organization development consultant with a large public utility.

The third person, Tom Peck, had never held a job in the private sector before. He had a Ph.D. in management sciences and had consulted in both the private and public sectors for a number of years. His focus, both academic and in consultation, had been on the issues of organization design.

Don's desire in bringing these three people together was to make possible a systemic approach to his department's assignment. Ed possessed experience in strategic planning; Gail's training was in individual and group interaction; and Tom had a strong background in organization design. Between them, they possessed expertise in the definition of long- and short-term organization objectives (the essence of the "functional" approach); the facilitation of employee participation (the essence of the "process" approach); and the improvement of unit/department/division linkages and interactions (the essence of the "structural" approach). These three key perspectives are critical to improving the productivity of any organization.

OPPORTUNITY KNOCKS

After attending one of the initial quality department seminars, members of the OD Section strongly felt that they could contribute to the quality improvement effort. The corporate approach, at this point, focused mainly on defining what had to change and why. OD now possessed the expertise to help define in a comprehensive manner how to actually go about implementing the desired changes.

The first step was to develop a model and to test it. The opportunity to do so came through the joint efforts of Don and Ed. The manager of the Eastern Mill, one of Core's largest primary mills that produced both pulp and paper products, had begun a project to develop a state-of-the-art finishing, storing, and shipping (PS&D) division. To identify the changes necessary, he had decided to form a task force from internal corporate consultants with the necessary technical expertise. When Don, who had held a series of conversations with the manager, suggested that Ed be made part of the task force, the mill manager consented.

The initial meetings were held shortly thereafter. When Ed suggested that the employees themselves be asked to offer improvements, some of the internal technical consultants objected strongly. The mill manager, however, decided that the two approaches—consultant driven and employee driven—should be mounted simultaneously.

Ed's (OD's) assignment was to review, with input from PS&D staff, all possible organization structures suitable to PS&D; to define the strengths and weaknesses of each; and to examine the current PS&D communications system and suggest ways to improve it. This assignment fit well with OD's objectives. It gave the department access to PS&D employees. It provided as a twin focus the division's structure and its communication system.

THE APPROACH

Beck at Core, the OD Section staff began putting together the model to be used at the Eastern Mill. At this point, all it actually had was a set of systems concepts agreed upon during earlier staff meetings. As a starting point, it was decided that in all businesses, two types of problem solving occur. The first was labeled "operational." This involved everyday issues that affected the mill's ability to survive and that required immediate attention. The focus was on getting the daily requirement of sheets, rolls, and so on, out the door. Operational problems were usually generated by the production process itself—sudden machine or computer stoppages, the loss of orders, and sick or negligent employees. Corporations locked into "crisis management" are usually those that cannot get beyond operational problem solving.

The second type of problem was labeled "design related." This included efforts by employees on all levels to improve the operation based on their experience and ideas. Design-related problems and improvements did not usually require immediate attention. Examples included discovering the best way to shorten an operating procedure, developing a more effective training program, and improving an interface between shifts or departments.

A love-hate relationship existed between operational and design-related problem-solving efforts. On the love side, design related problem-solving efforts helped reduce the need for operational problem-solving efforts. While the operational efforts were short-term in perspective and focused on keeping things going, the design-related efforts were longer-term in perspective and focused, at least partially, on decreasing the number of daily operational problems that had to be addressed. Obviously, everyone was in favor of making as many design-related improvements as possible.

On the hate side was the fact that these two types of activity competed for time and resources, with operational problem-solving efforts necessarily winning out. All supervisors wanted to work on design-related improvements. First, however, they had to deal with the mechanical problem causing a slowdown, then with an employee's drinking problem, then with a critical shortage of replacement parts, then with an unhappy customer, and so on.

Once the hate side of the relationship was understood, it was not difficult to figure out why employees gave up suggesting improvements. It was also easy to figure out why so many corporations were beginning to suspect that long-term planning was mainly a waste of time.

THE MODEL

With the above in mind, the OD staff shaped a model for the Eastern Mill that had five key characteristics. The first was that it segregated, at least initially, design-related problem-solving efforts from operational problem-solving efforts. This was necessary if the former were to receive adequate attention. A network of teams would be formed. These teams would meet for one hour a week, during which time they would focus solely on systemic improvements.

The second key characteristic was that the team building effort would begin in the hourly ranks. As quickly as possible, hourly employees would be given the chance to make reasonable changes in their areas of expertise.

A third key characteristic was that, while team building would begin from the bottom up, top-level management would also play an immediate role in the process. If possible, a planning exercise should be started. The lead team should put together an "idealized" version of the PS&D division that would provide a framework for the improvements coming from the hourly teams. Such participation would, in all probability, be a learning experience for top-level managers. It would also subtly demonstrate the need to expand the project mill-wide. Finally, it would make top-level management more accessible to the QIP teams as the two efforts began to mesh.

The fourth characteristic concerned the role of the OD consultants. Their role would be to make sure that all employees developed an accurate understanding of the approach; to help gain the support of upper-level management, specifically the mill manager; to bring up the teams; and, most important, to train and organize a network of facilitators, who would be responsible for maintaining the teams once the OD consultants left. A head facilitator would be appointed by the mill manager and would work with the OD consultants to help plan and guide the overall effort. An obvious candidate for this role was the mill head of human resources.

The fifth characteristic was that the team network needed to be effectively integrated. A way had to be developed to deal with problems affecting more than one team, to avoid repetition of effort, and to keep the teams informed of what others were doing so that they might maintain a division-wide and mill-wide perspective.

The OD staff designed a layered system that would help assure the required integration (see Figure 4.1). The lowest level would be composed of hourly teams representing key functions within each division. The second level would include one team for the PS&D division and one for each of the other divisions if they eventually became involved. Representatives from the hourly teams would make up this team, as would division supervisors. This team would address issues that crossed hourly team boundaries. A third-level team would exist if the process eventually went mill-wide. On it would be representatives from all division (second-level) teams as well as superintendents. The third-level team would address issues that crossed division boundaries.

Figure 4.1
The Quality Improvement Processes Team Network Model Designed for the Eastern Mill Process

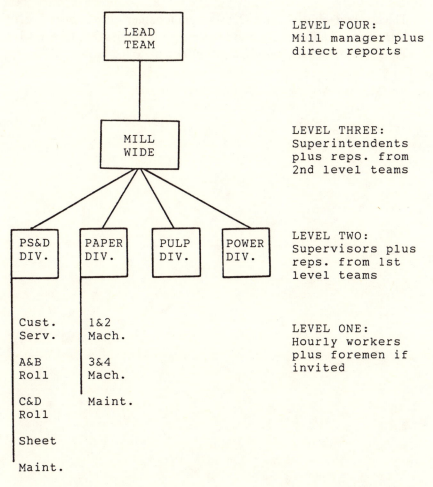

```
                    ┌──────────┐          LEVEL FOUR:
                    │  LEAD    │          Mill manager plus
                    │  TEAM    │          direct reports
                    └──────────┘

                    ┌──────────┐          LEVEL THREE:
                    │  MILL    │          Superintendents
                    │  WIDE    │          plus reps. from
                    └──────────┘          2nd level teams

  ┌──────┐  ┌──────┐  ┌──────┐  ┌──────┐  LEVEL TWO:
  │ PS&D │  │PAPER │  │ PULP │  │POWER │  Supervisors plus
  │ DIV. │  │DIV.  │  │ DIV. │  │DIV.  │  reps. from 1st
  └──────┘  └──────┘  └──────┘  └──────┘  level teams

   Cust.     1&2                          LEVEL ONE:
   Serv.     Mach.                        Hourly workers
                                          plus foremen if
   A&B       3&4                          invited
   Roll      Mach.

   C&D       Maint.
   Roll

   Sheet

  Maint.
```

The lead team would be composed of the mill manager and his or her direct reports. It would have three responsibilities:

1. To become directly involved in projects concerning major outside stakeholders, such as corporate headquarters, suppliers, and so on;

2. To review proposed improvements involving corporate policy changes or large sums of money, contributing input and a "go" or "no-go" decision when necessary;

3. To develop a long-term plan for the mill and lead a mill-wide
   redesign effort based on that plan.

The last two things that the OD staff put together were a general set of
action steps and a first draft of the process ground rules (see Chapter 3).
Thus armed, the OD consultants headed back to the Eastern Mill.

CHAPTER 5

Getting the Ball Rolling

SETTING THE STAGE

After gaining the mill manager's acceptance of their proposed action steps, the OD consultants met with the head of the mill's human resources department to break down the PS&D division by function. The categories decided upon were customer service, roll finishing machine A, roll finishing machine B, sheet finishing, and maintenance. Roll finishing A and B each included 50 to 60 employees, as did sheet finishing. Maintenance included 30 employees. Teams of 10 to 12 hourly workers would represent these five functions.

An alternative would have been to break down the work force according to shift and across functions. A strength of the shift approach would have been improved communication between the major operations in PS&D. Another would have been ease of scheduling team meetings and of assuring attendance. A weakness, however, would have been the range of concerns that representatives of the related but technically different operations would have wanted to address. Would enough common problems exist? If not, would the team members be interested in each other's problems? Which unit's problems would take precedence? Finally, would the team members not directly involved in the improvement currently being discussed lose interest?

The major strength of breaking down the teams according to function would be commonality of interest. Also, each function would have the chance to "get its own sandbox in order" before addressing its relationship with other functions. In terms of improving communication, a great number of the problems and misunderstandings that existed between shifts could be dealt with immediately when the teams included representatives from all four. The challenge of this approach would be getting team members together when they worked at three different times during the day and night.

The mill manager supported the decision to form the teams around functions. If this arrangement didn't work, it could be changed, but he was fairly sure that it would work. Team members would not volunteer, at least not initially. They would be appointed by the foremen and supervisors and would be required to attend meetings, even during off hours, until they understood what the process had to offer. If they eventually felt that they had no contribution to make or remained highly dissatisfied with the loss of one hour a week of work or free time, a substitute could be found. Those coming in during off hours would be paid overtime for the time spent in meetings. Foremen and supervisors were instructed to choose the employees that they thought capable of making contributions in terms of both experience and attitude.

The question arose of whether maintenance should have a team of its own or whether representatives should act as a resource to the other divisional teams. With input from the heads of PS&D and maintenance, it was eventually decided that this function should have its own team and should deal initially with issues internal to its own operation. This arrangement would allow maintenance personnel to concentrate first on their own procedures and equipment needs. It would allow them also to design, from their own perspective, the desired relationship with the storeroom and the production units they served before involving other stakeholders.

At the same time, ground rules 8 and 9 guaranteed the rest of the teams access to members of the maintenance crew on an as-needed basis (see Chapter 3). This arrangement would prevent time from being wasted. Maintenance personnel would not have to sit and listen to members from, say, the sheet finishing team discuss issues in which they played no role.

The next point brought up was whether or not foremen or other supervisors should be made members of the hourly teams. Corporate policy was that they should. A major purpose of the team building effort was to improve relations between the hourly work force and management. Having the two sides join together in a problem-solving effort was a step in this direction.

The OD consultants disagreed. The most important purpose of the team building process was to increase the commitment of the total work force to improved quality. This could be done on the hourly level by showing workers that management respected and desired their input and ideas. The teams were a vehicle for encouraging them to speak up. If a foreman or supervisor was a team member from the start, however, it would be business as usual. The hourly workers would expect that person to take the lead and would be nervous about making suggestions that the foreman or supervisor might disagree with or find threatening. At the same time, the foreman would be put into an awkward situation. It would be difficult to give an opinion without appearing to attempt to dominate.

The ground rules insured management's input. But that input should be *invited* by hourly team members rather than forced upon them. They could eventually ask a popular foreman or supervisor to join the team, but the decision should be theirs.

Another point addressed by the mill manager before the process began was who the team facilitators should be. Mr. Dole felt strongly that young engineers should be used. The relationship between these people, frequently fresh out of school, and the more experienced mill hands and maintenance staff was not always good. Mr. Dole felt that the interaction resulting from making them hourly team facilitators would lead to an improvement in communication. It also would develop a better understanding on both sides of what the other had to offer.

Finally, the OD consultants observed that, in order to truly succeed, the team building process needed to be implemented mill-wide. The interdependencies that were bound to surface during problem-solving activities would make this necessary. Mr. Dole said that he understood but that the effort should proceed as scheduled. It should start with PS&D and see how things went.

THIS IS WHAT IT'S ALL ABOUT, FOLKS

The next step was to introduce briefly OD's approach to team building to top- and middle-level management. Because of his background in management sciences, Tom organized presentations for the mill manager's direct reports, union representatives, and superintendents and supervisors from PS&D. He began each presentation by talking about industry's growing realization that employee involvement was critical not only to increased competitiveness but frequently to survival. The old ways did not work anymore. There was too much to know in any modern operation for one person or a small group of people to have all the answers.

He then described the three traditional ways of involving employees on all levels in planning and problem-solving efforts—worker's councils, autonomous work groups, and quality circles. He discussed the strengths and weaknesses of each, then talked about the systems approach and how it incorporated them all. Finally, he presented the bottom-up model developed for the Eastern Mill. He stressed the point that once the introductory sessions were completed, the OD consultants would focus on bringing up hourly level teams. These people traditionally had been the most difficult to involve. They were the ones most prone to be left out of change efforts, most suspicious of management's motivation, and most skeptical about the seriousness of the effort and its chances of producing lasting change. At the same time, they were the ones, ultimately, upon whom success rested because they actually produced the pulp and paper.

The presentation to the mill manager's direct report was received in silence. No one said anything. No one asked questions. The presentation to the PS&D supervisors and superintendents brought the same response. One reason for the silence was that most attendees were in the presence of their immediate bosses. Tom talked about the current trend toward reducing middle-management staffing levels to cut costs and increase the efficiency of operations. He said that the OD model did not accept the logic behind this move. Too much valuable expertise was lost. The effect on overall employee morale was too great. The long-term negative consequences of such a tactic far outweighed the short-term positive ones. Instead, a new, more productive role for middle managers should be found. While a few members of the audience seemed to like what they were hearing and nodded approval, the majority stared blankly.

The presentation to the union representatives fostered an entirely different response. Numerous questions were asked. There were requests for elaboration. Finally, one representative said, "We've been asking for something like this for 20 years." Tom told the audience that the OD consultants would keep them fully informed about what was happening and would be available to answer any questions.

One question that came up in all three of these presentations was, "How much of the employee's time will these team meetings take?" The answer was that, following the start-up sessions, each team would meet weekly for an hour to an hour and a half until it has progressed far enough to set its own schedule. The second-level team meetings would consume an additional hour per week for representatives. The few employees on the third-level team would need a third hour each week for a meeting. It was pointed out that membership on all three team levels would rotate so that no one would constantly miss that much time.

MAIDEN VOYAGE

The OD consultants had, by this time, planned their strategy. Because of his organization design training and experience, Tom would take the lead in the team building effort. He would immediately begin training Ed and Gail in the necessary techniques. Hopefully, he would eventually be able to train several in-house people as well. Gail would function as chief trouble-shooter. Employees with serious doubts about the process would be directed initially to her. Gail would also provide "instant" training to meet process demands. If possible, she would let the mill's human resource staff and corporate training section handle requirements. When scheduling restrictions disallowed this alternative, however, she would design and lead the session personally. Ed would facilitate the lead team planning effort, if and when it started.

In terms of PS&D, the OD consultants decided to begin at the tail end of the operation and back into it for reasons discussed in Chapter 4. Based on this decision, the first team formed would be from the customer service department. This unit was responsible for scheduling paper production runs and for getting the finished product to customers. Because of the department's size, it was decided to include all hourly workers on the team. Mr. Dole agreed to close the office for the start-up exercise.

When the OD consultants arrived, the customer service staff was cheerful about getting time off from their normal duties but suspicious. Tom did not take time to explain the process, as he had for management levels and union representatives. He did not want to get bogged down answering questions.

Instead, he immediately led the customer service staff into a problem identification and prioritization exercise. He used a technique called a "search conference," which had been developed by Fred Emery. The group was asked to answer six questions:

1. What trend in the United States and your community are most affecting your quality of life?
2. What trends at Core as a whole are affecting your quality of working life?
3. What trends at the mill are affecting your quality of working life?
4. What trends with your own "25 square feet" are affecting your ability to do your job the way you want to do it?
5. What are your responsibilities?
6. What improvements would you suggest so that you can better meet your responsibilities as a department?

Table 5.1
First Start-up Session Notes for Customer Service

---

1. Trends in U.S./Community that Affect Quality of Life

- Exporting of jobs as industry moves out of country
- Bad exchange rate
- Immigrant labor taking jobs
- Growing national debt
- Growth of trucking industry, decline of rail use
- Rising personal taxes
- Good national governmental leadership
- Increased governmental involvement
- Decline in the quality of education
- Increase in drug, alcohol use due to:
  - —increasing stress
  - —poor judicial system
  - —peer pressure
- Decline in morality
- Young people want to help but lack leadership opportunities
- Greater competition overall
- Growing pressure, demands

2. Core Trends

- Diversification of Core into areas where we lack expertise
- Management wants more control over "little people"
- Management too rigid, lacks flexibility
- No back-up orders in system
- Crisis management, little time spent planning ahead
- Priorities undefined
- Must rely too much on corporate to get job done
- Lack of appropriate tools to get job done
- Rules not followed by everyone
- Poor communication systems overall:
  - —within mill
  - —between mills
  - —between mill and corporate
  - —within customer service department
- No coordinator at corporate
- Lots of buck passing
- Too many contacts at corporate

Table 5.1   *(continued)*

- Information necessary to job often unavailable or old, useless
- Bottlenecks in the information system
- People not answering phones/radios when called, not returning calls
- Data processing too far from customer service
- Warehouse too small, layout poor
- Every time more space becomes available, corporate fills it up
- No one responsible for the warehouse, no supervisor, paper stored all over the place, no pattern
- No delegation of authority
- No set pattern, no system
- Priorities change constantly
- Lack of technology—employees want it but also afraid
- Finishing department on low end of pay scale
- Engineers, etc., use mill as training grounds for other jobs
- Unskilled workers have little chance to improve situation
- Lots of dead-end jobs
- Lack of trust between management and work force
- Workers treated like schoolchildren
- Work load has increased
- Problems are kept secret, not allowed to talk about them. When they are solved, management solves them without letting anyone know what's going on

3.   Unit Trends (Customer Service)

- Too much supervision
- Lack of say in how to do job
- No positive feedback
- Physically crowded
- Communication poor because of partitions in office
- Volume of paperwork so great that it must be spread among three people, information not kept together
- New paperwork dumped on people to fill up "spare time"
- Useless work being done
- Performance measures not fair, poor performance frequently results from foul-ups in amendments, teletype messages, cross-referenced orders with different shipping dates not under the control of those being judged
- No real system for getting work done, crisis orientation
- No planning function

4.   Tasks

- Special projects

Table 5.1 *(continued)*

- Dispatch trucks
- Process orders
- Schedule shipments
- Prepare bill of lading
- Maintain inventory levels
- Revise ship dates
- Prepare late shipment reports
- Correspondence preparation
- Delete orders
- Filing
- Quality alters
- Provide information to corporate inside sales
- Match tallies
- Responsible to ship pool trucks
- Sheet backlog report
- Direct and maintain order shipment status
- Compile truckyard check
- Transmit telecopies and teletypes
- Receive and distribute orders/amendments
- Tally edit
- Mark off report
- Prepare cutter orders
- Prepare rewinder orders

5. Improvements

Level 1 (departmental)

- Shut door, stop people from using office as shortcut
- Put hold button on phones, install intercom/call commander
- Stop people from other departments from coming in and bothering us when we are working
- Regular breaks
- More filing cabinets
- Install word processor/provide training
- Do something about drafts in room
- Define work priorities
- Cross train
- Paint the office
- Get managers to provide all necessary information

Table 5.1 *(continued)*

Level 2 (divisional/PS&D)

- Improve communication with sheet room
- Develop passwords for gaining access to required information
- More training on new process control system

Level 3 (mill-wide)

- Interoffice porters
- Get key-punch machine
- Improve overall training system

Level 4 (involving key external stakeholders)

- Stop unnecessary calls from different places within company when desired information is already in the system
- Get five-day prior release for PM cycle (closed)
- Stop accessibility of all inside sales reps to system, establish coordinator
- Direct amendments to area of concern
- Make sure proper identification is on order changes
- Appoint a trim coordinator
- Give us 48-hour lead time concerning stock on hand
- Make sure the inventory level information we are given access to is accurate
- Improve communication on cycle changes

The first questions were nonpersonal, nonthreatening, general icebreakers. They were used to begin forming a relationship with the group. Gradually, the process became more focused. The definition of department responsibilities provided a frame of reference for problem identification. When it came time to suggest improvements, team members were told to mention anything that came to mind, regardless of whether the problem was just in their office, with another function, mill-wide, corporate-wide, or with an outside stakeholder, such as a trucking company.

A list of 29 issues evolved from this last question and were briefly discussed. They were then broken down according to four levels: (1) those that could be dealt with strictly by customer service staff; (2) those that involved another mill function; (3) those that were mill-wide; (4) those that required input from a major stakeholder outside the mill.

All six questions were covered during the first four-hour session. The results can be found in Table 5.1. During the exercise, participants had difficulty keeping Core and mill trends separate, so they were combined.

INTO THE TRENCHES

By the next day it was obvious that Tom had made a mistake in not explaining the team building process. A rumor had spread that the OD consultants were efficiency experts, and that their ultimate objective was to eliminate jobs. At the beginning of the next meeting, it was announced that the customer service team wanted union representatives present from this point on. Tom apologized for his shortsightedness, then proceeded to explain the process in detail. He stressed the point that because the team effort helped increase productivity, a successful process would most likely result in more rather than fewer jobs. The objective of the OD approach was to help improve the bottom line through better utilization of employee expertise rather than through the reduction of labor costs.

Team members, however, were not convinced, and eventually Mr. Dole had to be called in. When the demand for union representation on the team was voiced, he said absolutely not. The unions had been briefed as to what was planned and had said that they were willing to give it a chance. There was no need for a representative to attend.

The next step was to prioritize level-one issues, which were the most familiar and easiest to address. The customer service staff, however, argued that some of the issues from other levels were also of top priority (see Table 5.2). Tom said, "Fine. It's your team. Give it a shot. But we don't want to become immediately involved in a project that's going to take months. Our objective is to show quick results. We want to prove to ourselves that we can create change. We want to show management the value of the team approach."

Table 5.2
Second Start-up Session Notes for Customer Service

Priorities (Not in Order)

- Develop an adult atmosphere in the office
- Gain the necessary knowledge and expertise with the new process control system
- Define our job priorities and responsibilities and give us access to the information we need
- Get two signs made to put on office doors ("No Thru Traffic")
- Get additional file cabinets
- Install a call commander or put hold buttons on phones

PRIORITY PROJECT 1

Departmental communication was then selected as the number-one priority project. Team members felt that they frequently lacked the information that they needed access to, and that their job priorities and responsibilities were often not well enough defined. PS&D had two supervisors, the department head and his assistant. These two were isolated physically from the rest of the staff in their own offices and were frequently unavailable.

As an initial step, the team wanted to invite the department head and his assistant to the meeting. When they arrived, however, no one spoke. Tom was forced to present the project list and to explain the first priority. When the senior manager asked what was wrong with department communication, someone finally said that the staff was tired of being treated like kids. The department head retorted that they were treated like kids because they acted like kids.

Tom guided the team into defining systemic ways to improve the situation. Allowing the personal issue to surface had been necessary. But permitting participants to dwell on it would not have been as productive as encouraging the team to address the problem as a systemic rather than a personal one.

Within an hour the group had generated a list of five ways to improve departmental communication. Also, team members had agreed to begin writing their own job descriptions. At this point the managers had to leave for another meeting. Following their departure, the hourly workers decided that the department head and his assistant should be invited to attend team meetings on a regular basis.

PRIORITY PROJECT 2

The second priority addressed was training on process control systems. The two systems involved were new. They had been installed by corporate experts. These people had then spent several days training customer service department users. When these experts left, however, and the trainees had actually begun using the new technology to schedule machine runs and integrate mill-wide operations, a great number of questions and doubts had arisen. Users admitted that at present they were frequently guessing at procedures. In other instances, they used the new system, then repeated the procedure on the old one as a check. Finally, some were simply ignoring the new system and depended entirely on the old one.

The facilitator selected for this team by Mr. Dole, a young engineer, had joined the second session. Her instructions were to sit and watch, becoming familiar with the team's problem list, priorities, and the way that Tom facilitated the team's efforts. However, when team members began explaining their doubts about the process control system, she grew alarmed. The entire mill operation was affected by what customer service fed into this system. She asked, "Why haven't you called the corporate experts with your questions?" Some team members replied that they had been afraid to do so. Others said that they had tried to call but, due to the experts' travel schedules, had encountered difficulties in reaching people with the right answers.

The facilitator said that she would take care of the problem immediately. Tom interrupted to tell her that problem solving wasn't her role. It was a team project. Team members should make the contact. But first, one of the ground rules had to be honored, the one about involving everyone directly affected. Who would that be? The team responded that everyone in the mill was affected. This was a third- and maybe even a fourth-level problem. Tom asked where they thought they should start in terms of involvement. Team members said that they should first approach their own supervisors.

The facilitator invited the two men to join the meeting once more. Both were greatly disturbed by what they heard. The department head asked why staff members hadn't posed their questions when the experts were on site. Team members responded that they hadn't known the questions at that point. The department head said that he would take care of the problem immediately. Again, Tom said, no, it was a team problem now. The team would deal with it but needed his support and input.

When the department manager left, his assistant stayed and said that he would like to join the team if possible, that the department head didn't communicate well with him either. That's why he hadn't been of more use to the hourly workers. If the team process could help change that one relationship, it would produce a great improvement.

Other key stakeholders in terms of this issue were the PS&D division superintendent and top-level management. The assistant manager of the department said that he would discuss the problem with the division superintendent. Because team members were hesitant at this point to address top-level management, not knowing what the reaction would be, the facilitator volunteered and was given that responsibility.

The next step was to generate project action steps. Tom asked the team to think in terms of an ideal scenario. What would members want to happen ideally? The answer was that an expert should be flown in again, not to give a presentation this time but to be available for as long as was necessary to answer questions and to help users develop the necessary familiarity with the system.

Unless other stakeholders disagreed, then, the first requirement was for someone to call corporate and request a return visit by an expert. Team members balked. They said that they didn't have the authority to make such a call. Tom insisted. It was their project. If it was going to be done, someone in the room would have to do it. Finally, one of the older employees volunteered. The facilitator said that she would help the volunteer reach the right person. The employee asked what she should do if no one would take her seriously. Tom answered that if the other mill stakeholders agreed with what was being done, the ground rules assured their support, right up to the mill manager.

A second action step defined by the team was for customer service personnel to begin compiling a list of questions to be sent in advance to the expert picked to visit so that he or she could prepare.

By the end of the session the team members were at least curious and seemed willing to give the process a chance.

The next stop for the OD consultants was the mill manager's office. There they suggested that the lead team planning exercise be started immediately to provide a frame of reference for problem-solving team efforts. Mr. Dole, however, said that it was too soon. His direct reports were not familiar with the "idealization" approach that was to be used. They needed to talk about it. They also needed to develop an understanding of the team problem-solving process. Finally, they needed to start solving some problems themselves, instead of having him always take the lead. This last comment was important. It showed Mr. Dole's realization that if the process were to succeed, he had to set the example by backing off and giving his direct reports more authority.

CHAPTER 6

Keeping Things Going

THE MILL MANAGER COMES THROUGH

The OD consultants returned to corporate. The plan was for them to spend two or three days each week at the mill during the initial phase of the process and two or three days at headquarters. Almost immediately, however, Gail began receiving calls from customer service team members at the mill. Things were not going smoothly. The two supervisors felt that they had been put on the spot without proper warning. They had complained to the PS&D division superintendent, who had supported them and had carried their complaint to the mill manager.

The supervisor who was the department head had also told the team that if it wanted to talk with him, two representatives should make an appointment and come to his office. He would then take whatever they said under consideration. Four team members, according to phone reports, had become physically ill following the consultants' departure. They were afraid of reprisals. They felt as though they had been put into a dangerous position, then deserted.

When the OD consultants arrived at the mill the following week, they talked initially with Mr. Dole. Then the consultants went to see the department head of customer service and his assistant, first to listen, then to review their role in relation to the team. Earlier in the week, Mr. Dole had made clear to the supervisors and to their superintendent that the team building process was not going to disappear, that they had to learn to live and work with it.

During this session the consultants suggested that when team issues were discussed, the two supervisors should meet with the entire team rather than just representatives. They suggested that such meetings be held in a more neutral location. Finally, they suggested that the supervisors not let the team dump problems into their laps. That was the old way. The team now had to be forced to take responsibility for discovering the best solutions and for implementing the action steps outlined.

The OD consultants then met with the team and reviewed its conversations with the department supervisors. One member wondered out loud if it was "worth the pain." The supervisors were eventually brought in, and the stakeholder involvement ground rule was reviewed to assure them that team members were not going to make important changes in department policy and processes without their input and consent.

ONWARD AND UPWARD

The next item on the meeting agenda was to discuss the progress of ongoing projects. Due to the confrontation, little had been accomplished. Action steps and assignments were reviewed. Because nothing more could be done on these first two priority projects until the current action steps had been completed, the team decided to move on to its third priority, the redesign of the flow of work through the office. It began identifying and seeking reasons for bottlenecks in this flow. One reason offered was job security. Employees were still traumatized by earlier "efficiency-increasing" studies. They felt that they could improve their chances of surviving the next cut by hoarding tasks and information.

The OD consultants explained that two approaches to improving the bottom line existed. The first was decreasing costs. In such cases, getting rid of employees was too frequently the easiest alternative. The second was finding ways to increase work-force productivity. The team was the nucleus of this second approach. If the team building effort produced the expected results, employment security should increase rather than decrease. In order for the team approach to work, however, members had to help each other, to share information and skills.

Team members then surprised the consultants by suggesting to the department head that his assistant be allowed to attend the daily meeting between himself and the PS&D superintendent. This way the assistant could help keep the team better informed. Both men seemed startled. Team members pressed their campaign, pointing out ways that the change would make his job easier and them more effective. Eventually, the manager said that he would see. It was also decided that the assistant should become a permanent team member. He could help keep the department manager and division superintendent informed of team activities.

One final issue addressed at this session was team notes. The ground rules stated that the team could decide to keep them private or to distribute them. If it picked the latter course, it had the right to decide who should get them. The consultants suggested that Mr. Dole be a major consideration. He had initiated the process and had protected the team. It was important to show him that the process was producing results. After much discussion and some pressure from the consultants, the team decided to distribute its notes to Mr. Dole but to no one else at this point.

TEAM TWO

During that same week, one of the roll finishing teams was formed. Workers in this function rewound paper from the large rolls coming off of the paper-making machines, cut it to size, and made up the smaller rolls that met customer specifications. Then they wrapped these smaller rolls and prepared them for shipment.

Due to the size of the roll finishing operation and the number of people involved—180—the OD consultants decided to form two teams—A/B shifts and C/D shifts. This decision contradicted the earlier one that all shifts in a function should be represented on one team. The consultants, however, wanted to involve as many people in the effort as possible. The decision gave them approximately 24 team members instead of 12. Also, the team building process was flexible. It was a learning experience for everyone. Nothing was carved in stone. If the arrangement didn't work, they could revert to a break down by function.

When the consultants met with shift foremen from roll finishing to introduce the process, the first comment they heard was, "This team concept is a bunch of crap!" After that, however, things went well. The foremen agreed that they had to deal with too many small, time-consuming, day-to-day problems, and that if they could get the hourly workers involved in handling some of these it would give them time to address larger issues. Everyone decided to give the team approach a chance. If it proved itself, fine. If not, it could be stopped by a wave of Mr. Dole's hand.

The idea of having two teams instead of one was presented. Meetings could be held at shift change-over, with representatives from the outgoing

Table 6.1
C and D Shift Roll Finishing Team's Improvements/Priorities

Level 1

- None

Level 2

- Reorganize training
- Define position responsibility clearly
- Balance work load
- Standardize procedures between shifts
- Stop competition between shifts
- Proper equipment and proper quantities
- Each area properly equipped
- Shifts share equipment
- Improve communication with order department
- Designate inventory area in warehouse
- Need short boom tow motor
- Need more dependable equipment
- Relocate tally shack
- Need tally printers in all shipping shacks
- Need cleanup people to increase productivity
- Need recognition when job well done
- Create an adult, trusting environment
- Reinstitute position of head roll finisher
- Plan ahead to match available transportation with production
- Get skill saw to cut boards to brace trucks and rail cars

Level 3

- Reestablish chain of command
- More recent reference sheets
- Coordinate production of roll sizes
- Replace large rewinder
- New roll wrapper
- Assign maintenance to department from 4 P.M. to 8 P.M.
- Need noise control for shredder
- Reduce overruns when making rolls
- Make sure we get accurate input cards
- Improve communication and cooperation between winder and roll finishing

Table 6.1 *(continued)*

- Purchase and install banding machine
- Develop unit strictly for the maintenance of PS&D tow motors

Level 4
- Make "crew concept" work or replace it
- Control inventory levels, think "just in time" not "just in case"
- Curtail last-minute changes in shipments
- Supply trucks "just in time" instead of backing them up in the yard

Priorities
1. Reorganize training
2. Create an adult, trusting atmosphere
3. Balance the work load
4. Designate inventory areas in the warehouse
5. Equip each area properly
6. Reinstate head roll finisher

---

shift staying an extra hour. The foremen asked if those staying the extra hour would be paid overtime. Ed told them of Mr. Dole's decision that they would. The foremen said that the alternative—having all four shifts represented on one team—would never work. Those sleeping or not working that day or night would never come in.

In the first start-up session with roll finishing shifts C and D, the consultants explained what the team building process was for; how it worked; the results hoped for; how it probably would improve employment security; and the ground rules.

A search conference was then run. Ed took the lead in guiding the team through its definition of desired improvements. The breakdown of these improvements, according to the team level that would need to address each and the definition of priorities, is found in Table 6.1. Ed introduced a simple technique for defining priorities. Each team member would call out his or her top three. Ed would give the choices one, two, or three points. The priority that ended up with the greatest number of points would become number one, and so on. If a tie occurred, there would be discussion, then another vote.

KEEPING THE MILL MANAGER UP TO SPEED

Before heading back to corporate, the consultants visited the mill manager again. By this time, he had received session notes from customer service and was surprised that staff wanted more training on the process control system. He said that he would make the necessary calls immediately. The consultants had to work hard to convince him not to "jump the process." Mr. Dole eventually shook his head and said that it seemed like the long way around. But, on the other hand, if the team hadn't brought the problem out, it could have festered for months. This was, indeed, a new way of doing things, but he would try to adjust.

The consultants explained that when only one or two teams were involved and one or two projects were being worked on, the process was inefficient in terms of time. But when 50 or 60 teams were working on several hundred projects, the payback in terms of time and efficient use of resources would be great. A little patience at the start would produce tremendous benefits in the long run.

The second issue discussed at this meeting was employee security. So long as employees suspected that they might be fired tomorrow during an efficiency purge, fostering the degree of commitment necessary to the process would be difficult. Though corporate was constantly pressuring the mills to reduce numbers, was there anything that Mr. Dole could do to alleviate his people's fears? They respected him as a person of his word. If he could come up with something. . . . Mr. Dole said, yes, he understood the problem and would work on it.

Finally, Mr. Dole brought up the issue of task forces. There were projects that needed to be started in PS&D. Did management have to wait for the teams to identify and choose to work on them? The answer was no. Management was free to start any project it wanted, to build any task force, and to include any QIP team members that it wished. The "design-related," problem-solving, team network approach being developed by the OD consultants was *not* supposed to replace normal operational problem-solving procedures but to complement them.

At the same time, however, management could not use the hourly teams, at least initially, to do jobs it thought important. The teams *had* to be allowed to identify their own priorities if the desired degrees of ownership and commitment were to be fostered. One thing that made this arrangement easier to accept was that more often than not team priorities matched those of management.

THE THIRD WEEK

By the following week, a lot was going on at the mill. Mr. Dole had found space for team meetings in an old training building that sat away from the mill. The OD consultants had requested such an area, which was free from distractions, that the teams could eventually claim as their own. It was a bit of a walk, but this provided a small break—a transition period for workers coming off of their jobs.

The facilitator ran the fourth meeting of the customer service team with an OD consultant sitting in support. The meeting was spent reviewing action steps in process on priority projects and identifying new projects (see Table 6.2). Team members were beginning to believe that they could make things happen. For example, the assistant department supervisor had been invited to attend morning meetings with the department supervisor and the division superintendent.

Much of the fear was gone, replaced by cautious enthusiasm. It was quickly becoming obvious that most of the actual work on these projects would be done during the week. Team meetings would mainly review ongoing activities and the planning of future ones.

Most of the priorities picked by the C/D shift roll finishing team had been second level. It was pointed out that the second-level team, which would deal with such problems, had not yet been formed. The C/D shift

Table 6.2
Customer Service Session Four Notes

---

1. Make process control system training mandatory for everyone in the department.
   - Bring in trainer from corporate
   - Make upper-level management aware of need
   - Work with each other to improve understanding
2. Put order in for "No Thruway" signs for doors.
3. Develop justification for "floater" to cover illnesses, vacations.
4. Discuss paperwork excesses with stakeholders in other departments.
5. Develop individual lists of training we need, training we can offer each other.
6. Find way to get a copy of roll shipping information earlier.
   - Should be retrievable from system
   - "Window" needed at corporate

---

team, however, decided not to change its priorities. It would, instead, work on the presentation of its number-one concern to the second-level team. This was acceptable because the initial action step taken to develop such a presentation was a problem analysis, and such analyses frequently ended up redefining the problem in such a way that the team could address parts of it without getting other stakeholders involved.

The issues this group had chosen to address included: the training and cross-training of shift workers; the reinstitution of a head role finisher, a position cut out as a result of the corporate efficiency thrust; and the availability of tools to all sections and shifts.

In terms of the second issue, it was pointed out that according to the ground rules, the team had to show the reinstitution of this position to be economically beneficial to the mill. It had to develop a believable cost-benefit analysis balancing the salary of the extra position against the loss of efficiency caused by others on the shift having to handle that position's responsibilities in addition to their own. The team said that such an analysis would be difficult to put together. The OD consultants said, true, but this was how the game was played. The ground rules also asserted that any proposed change had to have the approval of all affected, and upper-level management, as such a stakeholder, wasn't going to reverse a corporate staff decision without good reason.

In terms of the third issue, the OD consultants pointed out that the availability of tools for crew members was always a problem in primary manufacturing operations, that when made available they tended to disappear. The only way that team members were going to convince management to provide more was to say that the team or the shifts represented could and would take responsibility for the tools not "walking."

The team decided to focus on this issue during its next meeting. It also decided that it would be to the team's benefit to release meeting notes to anyone interested, from the mill manager on down. The major mill-wide problem, in the team's opinion, was lack of appropriate communication, and this was one way of addressing it.

ROLL FINISHING SHIFTS A AND B

Ed ran the entire start-up exercise for the third team formed, roll finishing shifts A and B, with Tom and Gail observing. Possibly because members had talked to their coworkers on shifts C and D, this team became involved without any hesitation. By the start of the second session, it had already defined its priorities and was set to begin solving problems. Most of the issues identified were the same as those identified by the C/D team. Its priorities are listed in Table 6.3.

Instead of beginning the problem-solving process with an analysis of its first three priorities, it was suggested, as an experiment, that the A/B team idealize. It should start by identifying the characteristics that each system ought to possess ideally rather than each system's faults. The results of this approach can be found in Table 6.4

The team's fourth priority—"knowledge of the new process control system"—was the result, mainly, of fears about the new system eliminating jobs. Instead of idealizing, members generated a list of questions for the mill manager and the expert from corporate to answer while the expert was working with the customer service staff (see Table 6.5).

The issue of releasing meeting notes was brought up at that point. The team, following the lead of C and D shifts, decided to release them to anyone interested, so long as individual comments were not included and opinions and decisions were presented as those of the team as a whole. It was explained to the team that this need to protect individual team members and their opinions was one reason that decisions were reached through consensus rather than vote. A second reason was that until everyone accepted it, the most workable solution had not yet been achieved. A third was that it was more efficient to spend the time up front fostering the required level of commitment and understanding than it was to try to do so during the implementation phase. Again, in terms of reasons 2 and 3, the ground rules made it impossible for teams to act otherwise.

From that point on, all new teams decided to release their meeting notes to anyone interested. A distribution list was developed, including the mill manager, his direct reports, and everyone in the management hierarchy of

Table 6.3
A and B Shifts Roll Finishing Team Priorities

1. Knowledge of new process control system.
2. Improvements in training.
3. Better use of people.
4. Problem solving instead of pressure.
5. Modification of "crew concept."
6. Improvement of shipping system.
7. Improve and maintain equipment.

Table 6.4
A and B Shifts Roll Finishing Team Definition of Ideal Characteristics for the Systems Addressed by Its First Three Priorities

---

1. Pressure Versus Problem Solving

- Should have one boss, reestablish chain of command
- First ask operators what problem is, then solve it together
- Don't blame us or just tell us, work with us
- Adult atmosphere
- Management should stop assuming we're goofing off, that we don't care about our jobs

2. Training

- Should be more on the job
- Should be led by experienced operators
- Properly trained back-up people should be in place
- Consistent training schedule should be developed
- Proper training should be received before starting job
- Should be ongoing
- Training program should be flexible, some learn faster, some need more training than others
- Same trainer should be used over time
- Instead of using spare time to clean up, paint, etc., use it to train
- Stop cancelling vacations because not enough trained people

3. Crew Concept

- Rotation schedule should be consistent—rotate every four weeks
- Rotate one group at a time—not the whole shift simultaneously
- There should be more consistent movement upward
- Train people before promoting them
- Redistribute key people with the necessary training so that more of us have access to them
- Let workers know how the decision as to who rotates is made

---

Table 6.5
Questions Concerning New Process Control System

- How many jobs will be affected?
- Which jobs will be affected and how?
- What is going to happen to the people whose jobs are affected?
- How does the system work?

---

the individual team. Copies were also made available to hourly workers represented by the team.

The OD consultants next met with foremen from sheet finishing to brief them and to ask them to select team members for the following week's start-up session. The sheet finishing staff was small enough that one team seemed appropriate. The foremen already knew from the grapevine much of what was going to be said, and the meeting went smoothly.

During the squad's weekly exit meeting with Mr. Dole, he announced that the process should go mill-wide. He had received all team notes generated thus far and liked what he read. He was impressed that positive changes were already occurring. He had thought it would take much longer to get the hourly workers involved. Mr. Dole also said that a session should be set during the next visit to begin the long-range-planning exercise with his direct reports. Finally, the union presidents had called him and asked for a presentation. This should be scheduled as well.

CHAPTER 7

The Long Haul

WEEK FOUR

The fourth week of team building went according to plan. The customer service team had received approval for its project action steps from all stakeholders, including the mill manager. Between meetings, it had:

1. Contacted corporate about the need for more training on the process control system, sending along a list of questions. A trainer was scheduled to come in the next week and to stay as long as the team wished.
2. Sent a representative to talk to the mill manager about the need for a floater, one of the positions lost during the last efficiency study, presenting a rough cost-benefit analysis.
3. Picked their people for the second-level team.
4. Talked to a corporate expert about further automating their office, the types of equipment that would help improve efficiency, and how they could be integrated. The expert helped them over the phone and said that he would visit the mill soon.

Roll finishing C and D team members cancelled their week's meeting.

Table 7.1
A and B Roll Finishing Team Session Three Notes

Warehouse Problem Definition

1.   You can't stack orders together because not enough room.
2.   Area too strung out, loading docks are at north end and split.
3.   Can't find orders because they've been stacked wherever room can be found.
4.   Orders sometimes hidden behind other orders.
5.   Can't find orders because computer lies, says we have things that we don't, doesn't tell when something's been shipped.
6.   Too many orders have to be stored, not enough shipped immediately.
7.   Poor communication with paper machines, customer service.
8.   Computer goes down almost daily.
9.   Too much bad paper coming down, someone up the line is trying to meet his production quota no matter what.
10. No one is in charge of the warehouse, everyone you go to has a different answer.
11. Need 24-hour switching to move trucks in and out of loading docks.
12. Need another tow motor driver to haul from one area to another.

Roll finishing A and B team had decided to make the reorganization of the warehouse its first priority project. During A and B's meeting, a problem analysis was done with a few suggested improvements thrown in (see Table 7.1). The team decided that the most important action step was to encourage upper-level management to give one individual responsibility for running the warehouse and for setting and enforcing policy. Currently, a number of supervisors had developed their own policies, especially concerning the allocation of space, and these policies often conflicted. The team decided to hand-distribute its meeting notes immediately to all stakeholders as a means of making sure that they became aware of the seriousness of the problem and of the team's suggestions.

A and B shift team members also decided that they needed to meet with representatives of the C and D shift team. A great number of the issues that interested them involved all four shifts. When asked, however, if they wanted to combine the two teams, the answer was, no, they didn't want to dilute their effort. They wanted to continue working on the warehouse and other priorities by themselves. A third team, including representatives from all shifts, should be formed to deal with cross-shift issues.

SHEET FINISHING

Gail ran the two-day start-up for the sheet finishing team, which included representatives from all shifts with Ed sitting in support.

Next, Ed introduced the long-term planning phase of the process to Mr. Dole's direct reports and to several other managers who had been added to the group to make up a "lead team." The plan was for Mr. Dole to facilitate this team. Ed started with a presentation on the concept of idealization. When he asked for questions, there was no response. In fact, during the entire session, only one person other than Ed and Mr. Dole spoke.

Back in Mr. Dole's office, it was suggested that Ed stay with the team and play the role of both facilitator and consultant until momentum had been gained. It was also suggested that Mr. Dole miss the next several meetings for the same reason that foremen and supervisors were asked to stay away from the initial meetings of problem-solving teams. Mr. Dole accepted the recommendations.

WEEK FIVE

During the fifth week, the hourly PS&D maintenance team and the joint roll finishing team were formed. The maintenance start-up was run entirely by Gail. Some of the old-time maintenance workers were extremely skeptical. One eventually said, "This thing will last six months, then will be gone, like everything else that corporate sends down. Somebody up there is just trying to get a little attention." Two other older team members spent the entire first meeting staring blankly at the wall. The younger workers, however, got involved quickly. One thing that everyone seemed pleased about was the fact that maintenance personnel had been given a team of their own instead of being made part of other teams.

Tom started the joint A and B shift/C and D shift roll finishing team. No one knew what to expect. The team began by listing problems that would affect all four shifts, then prioritizing them. Its top three priorities were the warehouse, training, and tools. This confused things even more. In terms of the warehouse, for example, who was going to take the lead in the project—the joint team or the A and B shift team, which was already working on it?

The joint team was encouraged to change its priorities and to focus, instead, on finding ways to improve cooperation between shifts. The team agreed and started by listing things that the individual shifts could do to improve relations. The list included: clean up after themselves, share tools, stop competing, and stop leaving work undone.

Table 7.2
Facilitator Responsibilities

---

1. Make sure ground rules are understood and obeyed.
2. Have team review prioritized projects and action steps taken.
3. Have team discuss new action steps to be taken.
   - Make sure responsibilities are assigned to team members.
   - Make sure timetable established.
   - Have team discuss desired results.
4. Help teams define and gain access to desired resources.
5. Have team discuss new projects suggested by employees represented and add to list.
6. Have team define new priorities when projects are completed or dropped.
7. Make sure someone takes notes.
8. Schedule next meeting and write on calendar.
9. Set up system for rotating membership.

The team decided, as its first action step, to design and begin an awareness campaign. If this didn't work, it would set up task forces around the individual issues.

Customer service and the C and D roll finishing team had, by this time, completed projects. Customer service had:

1. Acquired additional filing cabinets.
2. Made up and posted the desired "No Thruway" signs on its office doors.
3. Begun its process control system training with the expert from corporate.
4. Received an on-site presentation from a corporate office automation equipment expert concerning what existed and what would be most appropriate for the department's situation.
5. Received missing manuals for the process control system.

The C and D shifts team had:

1. Finished an inventory of tools that the shifts had access to and needed, then developed a system for safeguarding them.
2. Developed a system for returning damaged rolls to the rewinders.

The PS&D department now had three facilitators. All were young engineers. Each would work with two teams. Facilitator responsibilities were drafted by the OD consultants and reviewed by the new facilitators (see Table 7.2).

It was also decided at this point that teams should choose their own meeting times. Facilitators would be responsible for arranging their schedules so that they could be available. The teams, however, decided that their facilitator's work load, as well as their own, should be taken into account when making this decision.

THE MILL MANAGER BUYS IN

This time, the end-of-the-visit meeting with Mr. Dole was an especially lively one. He said that he continually had to fight the urge to get directly involved, to solve the problems himself. An example was the inventory problem and the desire expressed by the roll finishing C and D team to switch to a just-in-time system instead of constantly stockpiling. Mr. Dole said that the answer to this one was simple. Corporate policy made the Eastern Mill responsible for maintaining specific inventory levels, not for meeting orders.

The problem, as he saw it, was not that the policy was bad but that the team did not understand it. In fact, after looking through team notes, Mr. Dole said that he had realized that at least 70 percent of the issues raised by the teams were partially the result of a lack of appropriate understanding. It was obvious that communication and education had to improve mill-wide. He hadn't known that the hourly workers were truly interested in knowing these things.

In his own case, he couldn't believe that he had just found out that no floor plan or agreed-upon allocation of storage space existed in the warehouse. He was also surprised to learn that team members thought that no one was in charge. A supervisor, indeed, had the warehouse as one of his responsibilities.

When Mr. Dole was informed that the supervisor in question had been contacted and had reported that his decisions concerning the warehouse were constantly being overridden by superiors, Mr. Dole asked if he was allowed to get involved as a stakeholder. The answer was yes. The C and D roll finishing team had defined the problem as members saw it, then distributed its ideas to those who needed to play a role in the improvement effort, including Mr. Dole. There was nothing more the team could accomplish without his intervention. If Mr. Dole would inform the originating team of his intentions and involve it as a stakeholder in the improvement effort, everyone would probably be pleased.

Before departure, one final observation was made concerning Mr. Dole's comment about the need for improved communication. The formation of the team network was, in essence, a communications vehicle. The ground rules insured this. It forced focused and well-integrated communication in all directions regarding the issues addressed. The main purpose of the team building process was not actually to generate improvements in the operation but to encourage a new openness in the mill management culture. Once people started communicating sufficiently, the improvements would take care of themselves.

WEEK SIX

Before the OD squad's return in the sixth week, Mr. Dole had seen to it that one supervisor gained full responsibility for and the authority to run the warehouse. He had also formed a task force to allocate the space. Representatives from all the PS&D department teams were on the task force.

The agenda for the sixth week included a meeting with paper machine foremen and starting the lead team planning exercise.

The visit was relatively uneventful. The PS&D department teams met on schedule. An OD consultant sat in on each meeting but contributed little. The facilitators by now understood their responsibilities and were gaining confidence in their new roles. The PS&D maintenance team had begun work on its first priority project—misuse of the work order system—by generating a list of the system's desired characteristics and another list of questions that needed to be answered concerning it (see Table 7.3).

The lead team met without Mr. Dole for its second session. The OD consultants announced that this exercise should also back into the mill so as not to preempt hourly team activities. Shipping would be the first function addressed. Ed, as facilitator, would follow the standard idealized design steps:

1. Define the mission of the shipping function in terms of all key stakeholder groups.
2. Identify key systems in the shipping area.
3. Define key characteristics each system should possess.

Table 7.3
PS&D Maintenance Team Work Order System Project: Desired Characteristics and Questions List

---

Characteristics

1. Everyone should be allowed to write work orders.
2. Foremen should sign off on all work.
3. Everyone should be trained to write work orders.
   - Foremen should be trained by maintenance planning.
   - Foremen should train shifts.
4. Eventually, work shouldn't be done without work orders.
5. Two key pieces of information are necessary.
   - What is the problem specifically?
   - Where is the problem located?

Questions

1. What should be written on work orders?
2. What is the procedure for submitting?
3. How should training on filling out and submitting work orders be organized?
4. When should work orders be written?
5. What should the approval level be?
6. How should an incentive system be set up to get work done as efficiently as possible?
   - The hourly wage system, in effect, encourages workers to draw the work out.

---

4. Identify systems design elements that would allow the function to gain these characteristics.
5. Identify stakeholders that the design must be discussed with and approved by before implementation begins.

The superintendent of PS&D expressed concern about all these people from other parts of the mill coming in to redesign his operation. Ed asked if the superintendent believed that they really understood what went on in his area. The answer was no. Ed asked if he believed that the development of such understanding would benefit his operation. The answer was yes. It was then suggested that he view the exercise as an opportunity to educate his peers. At the same time, because decisions were made by consensus, no changes would be allowed without his approval.

The exercise began with the identification of key stakeholders to the shipping function and with the development of a mission statement saying what the function should do or provide for each. Key systems were then identified. One, the truck dispatching system, was singled out as most needing improvement. The team then worked on defining the characteristics that it should possess ideally.

WEEK SEVEN

The OD consultants' agenda for the seventh week read as follows:

1. Third session for lead team.
   1.1 Continue PS&D idealization exercise, focus on the shipping function.
      - Develop scheduling system that allows turn-around time of 24–48 hours.
      - Idealize the system for choosing carriers.
      - Idealize the system for notifying carriers.
   1.2 Identify stakeholders who must change the way they do things, who must contribute to or be consulted on the lead team design.
2. Bring up second-level team in PS&D.
   2.1 List on a flip chart three priorities brought by each first-level team to the session.
   2.2 Have team representatives give a brief explanation of each priority.
   2.3 Combine similar priorities/projects.
   2.4 Identify the first-level teams that are stakeholders for each project.
   2.5 Have second-level representatives of these teams begin working on the project.
3. Give start-up presentations to the paper machine department's management corps, decide who will sit on the hourly teams in this department, schedule the first session for these teams, identify facilitators.
4. Sit in on at least some PS&D first-level team sessions to make sure that teams focus on and complete priority projects before starting others.
5. Try to get calendars put up in the meeting rooms on which facilitators can schedule team meetings.
6. Worry about too many things going on simultaneously in terms of meeting room space and OD section resources.

The overall mission of the shipping function had been defined by the lead team as "on-time delivery." The team continued working during this and the following week on the characteristics that shipping should possess ideally to fulfill its mission. The results of their efforts are found in Table 7.4

During this part of the exercise two things happened. First, the managers of other functions began asking questions and making statements like, "I

Table 7.4
Characteristics of Idealized Shipping Function

1. One person coordinating/supervising the effort per shift.
2. Up-to-date records of truck supply and paper inventory.
3. Low-cost carrier used.
4. Trucks loaded from dock closest to paper location.
5. Loaders have no trouble locating truck to be loaded.
6. Bracing of trucks/rail cars done efficiently.
7. Minimal reloading.
8. Shipping department maintains close contact with dispatcher.
9. Centralized shipping department.
10. One stop for carriers.
11. Computerized control of product location.
12. Computerized control of carrier pool and docking facilities.
13. All loaded trucks/vehicles inspected/verified to meet the mission of the function.

didn't know you did it that way." The second was that the team realized that it had to include other stakeholders, specifically trucking company schedulers and drivers, supervisors and hourly workers from shipping, and the customer service team, to understand whether the desired characteristics could be designed into the system or not. The team was encouraged to finish a "strawman" based on its own ideas, then to present it to the other key stakeholders so that their suggestions could be incorporated.

The second-level team for PS&D met and did what was proposed. Teams learned what the others were doing. As expected, however, confusion occurred when it came time to volunteer for projects. Many of the priorities brought to the team list were already being worked on at the first level or by a task force. Also, when more than one function wanted to become involved in a second-level project, the question arose as to how efforts would be coordinated.

The supervisors present, many of whom had ideas and priorities of their own, had not been given the opportunity to contribute to the list. They didn't know what their role was supposed to be, whether or not they were allowed to make suggestions. They also worried about the additional time spent by hourly workers in second-level meetings

Finally, representatives from the different functions were interested mainly in their own second-level priorities and grew restless while others were being discussed. The meeting ended without clear assignments having been made. A weekly session was agreed upon, but the question remained of whether or not this was the best vehicle for dealing with the broader problems identified by the teams and for getting middle-level managers involved in the process.

The first-level teams visited were all immersed in projects. Customer service was pricing word processors as well as the equipment necessary for their recommended phone system modifications. The C and D team had developed a secured storage space for tools and spare parts and was waiting for the tools it had ordered to arrive. This team was also developing a form on which the reasons for roll rejects would be recorded. The A and B team was taking the lead in the warehouse reorganization. The joint roll finishing team was working on getting customer feedback on the condition of the rolls upon delivery.

In general, things seemed to be going well.

CHAPTER 8

Reward Time

PROCESS EVOLUTION

During a meeting at corporate, the OD section decided that, if possible, someone at the mill should be incorporated into the OD consulting group and trained so that hourly team members could have constant access to an on-site representative capable of addressing their questions and problems.

The head of mill human resources had too many other responsibilities. The squad's next choice was Mac Wills, maintenance training supervisor. Mac had begun attending the meetings of a variety of hourly teams and had volunteered to become a facilitator. Perhaps most important, however, he had worked at the mill for 23 years, knew everyone, and was liked by everyone.

Mac was pleased when asked, and Mr. Dole immediately okayed the suggestion. Mac's first assignment was to design display sheets to show each team's projects and their completion dates. The sheets would be hung in the entryway of the new meeting building.

During the eighth week, Tom, Ed, and Gail each brought up a paper machine area team. Mac attended most of the start-up sessions. The following two weeks were spent nurturing the new teams, working with the new facilitators, and striving to better integrate the team network. During this period, several critical issues were addressed. The first had to do with the lead team design exercise that encompassed the customer service function. The customer service team was upset. Once again bosses were planning its future without asking for input. This went directly against the process ground rules.

It was explained to customer service that the lead team was developing a strawman that customer service would then be asked to critique and to help modify. Customer service was not mollified. The issue of employee security had again reared its ugly head. This was a plot to get rid of jobs. By the time customer service was allowed to contribute to the design, it would be too late. The security issue had come up on other teams as well, the question being, "Will all these improvements make the operation so efficient that we lose our jobs?" It was becoming increasingly obvious that the OD consultants' assurances would not suffice. Something more concrete had to be offered by someone with real power.

The lead team decided to meet immediately with the customer service team and share its ideas. The first step in this direction was to generate a document that turned the already existing mission statement and characteristics for the shipping function into questions. For example, the mission statement of "on-time deliveries" was turned into the question, "Should be mission of the shipping function be simply to insure on-time deliveries?" In terms of characteristics, examples of the new format included, "Should the scheduling clerks cross-train so that they can support each other?" and "How can PS&D insure 24-hour notice to carriers?" Of course, many of the issues being addressed by the lead team were also on the customer service team's list, and many of the conclusions that the two teams had reached independently were similar.

Almost as soon as the two groups began talking, the fears of most of the customer service representatives dissolved, replaced by a feeling of pride that they were helping instruct the lead team and were being dealt with as equals while working on a joint project.

CLEARING THE WAY

A second critical issue resulted from the fact that several middle-level managers, especially the older ones, were having difficulty accepting the new culture. Some balked openly. Most of them, however, were simply sitting back and waiting quietly for it to go away. It was decided by the lead team and OD consultants that these people should not be confronted. They should be called on to provide information to teams and to function as stakeholders in projects affecting their part of the operation if they wanted to have a say. But nothing should be forced. As process momentum built and improvements piled up, most of them would eventually change their minds.

The logic behind this approach was that the process had to prove itself. If it produced results that improved their quality of working life and the operation as a whole, the doubters, as reasonable people, would come to understand and accept its value. The only requirement was that while they were waiting to be convinced, they, like everybody else, had to obey the ground rules. Mr. Dole's firmness with the PS&D superintendent and customer service supervisors had sent a very clear message that open resistance would not be tolerated.

MORE ISSUES

A third issue concerned work orders. Maintenance planners were receiving an increasing number of them, with the teams making the difference. They didn't like the fact that hourly workers were now allowed to write work orders. Maintenance was already overloaded. This just made the situation worse. Another question was, what kind of priority should team-generated work orders receive? Should they be considered equal in importance to or more important than those received through normal channels?

The lead team met with representatives of the maintenance planners. Mr. Dole explained that by the time a team-generated work order was written, all stakeholders, including supervisors and foremen, were supposed to have reviewed and approved the project. The immediate response was that in several known instances this had not occurred. The team had written an order without consulting anyone else.

The OD consultants said that this was going to happen. When hourly workers gained a new, attractive privilege, they tended to become defensive and to "jump" the process in order to protect their projects. It was the facilitator's responsibility, in such instances, to make the team retrace its steps and do things properly. When a supervisor suspected that a team was intentionally or unintentionally bypassing stakeholders, he or she should immediately inform the team's facilitator.

This was a learning process for everyone. The hourly workers had to understand that along with their new power, they must accept the responsibilities delegated by the ground rules.

Several members of the lead team then spoke in favor of the new, more open management system evolving. Mr. Dole said that the maintenance planners had to be patient and that they should give reasonable priority to team-generated work orders to demonstrate management's support of the team effort. The ground rule concerning response time did not mean that team-sponsored projects had to be scheduled within one week. It meant that those organizing the actual work needed to get back to the team with a "yes," a "no," or a "let's talk" within that period.

It was becoming increasingly obvious that Mr. Dole was *the* key actor in this effort. Without his strong backing too many ways existed to stifle the process. Up to this point, he had listened carefully to the OD consultants' recommendations and had said the right things to his work force. If he had questioned something, his reasoning had been good, and he had presented himself as a team member seeking the best solution rather than as a boss. Everyone in the mill was watching him. If he wavered, the OD consultants knew that many would back away in order to protect themselves and that those against the process would grow bolder in their attempts to scuttle it.

WEEK ELEVEN

By the eleventh week, approximately 50 projects had been undertaken by teams in the QIP network. An early concern had been that the workers would focus entirely on their own "comfort" issues. This did not occur. The majority of projects involved improvements in manufacturing and manufacturing support systems. In terms of product development, hourly workers, on their own suggestion, had begun visiting customers to discuss exactly what the customers wanted and how it could be achieved. In terms of management systems, due mainly to the process ground rules, greater amounts of information were being shared, channels were opening throughout the mill, and, slowly, increased input was being sought from more levels before decisions were made.

A typical project to improve the manufacturing process that concerned a supplier was undertaken by the sheet finishing team. Crews in the sheet finishing function operated a Will Sheeter, which cut, counted, stacked, wrapped, boxed, and palletized sheets of paper from rolls. The team was not satisfied with the cartons being supplied by another company. The team's problem analysis concluded that, because the cartons often carried different shades of coloration, had convex or concave surfaces, or were scored too deeply, the following was true:

1. The color differences were noticeable and unacceptable to a major customer.

2. The convex surface caused the machine to feed two to three cartons at a time and to jam.

3. Jamming in the carton machine slowed the sheeter and filled the accumulator belt. At times the jamming caused the machine to be stopped.

4. Concave cartons did not feed into the machine properly and, therefore, had to be hand fed.

5. When running convex and concave cartons, the operator had to tend to that machine only and could not complete other duties.

6. Cartons that were scored too deeply, especially carton bottoms, fell through the carton packing machine before it could set the bottom in place for packing. This caused the machine to jam.

The team worked on remedies for these issues. It then made a presentation to the lead team because this project involved a major outside stakeholder. The lead team's recommendation was that someone from the sheet finishing team contact the supplier and ask that representatives be sent to its next meeting. When this was done, the manager of the supplying company immediately telephoned Mr. Dole to find out what was going on. Mr. Dole said, "It sounds like my people want to talk. Why don't you send someone over?"

The following week, the manager of the supplying plant arrived himself, along with two of his reports. They went to Mr. Dole's office. Mr. Dole said, "Why don't you go on downstairs? The team's waiting." So the carton plant manager and his reports sat down with eight hourly workers and one foreman.

An OD consultant attended in support of the facilitator but said little while team members defined the problem, offered their ideas, and then worked for three hours with the visitors to generate solutions acceptable to all. By the end of the session the manager had established a hotline relationship between the team and his head of production to monitor progress.

ANOTHER TYPICAL PROJECT

Another typical project was undertaken by PS&D maintenance. It concerned a loading dock floor. The team's initial concern was tow motor repairs. Some of the vehicles seemed to spend most of their time in the shop. Team members began talking about causes of the seemingly excessive damage. Some of the drivers were hotdogging, but this was nothing new. Some needed more training. That could be dealt with but still did not seem to be the core problem. The team decided to go back through its records and find out what most of the repairs involved. The answer was loose clamp shafts, broken axles, ruptured tires, snapped chains, and out-of-line carriages. Next, team members spent time observing the operation. Almost immediately, the major cause of damage became obvious. Sections of the loading dock were heavily pocked. When a loaded tow motor hit one of these holes, it received a severe jolt.

The next step was to do a rough cost-benefit analysis. The team computed the normal yearly cost of the involved repairs. It then estimated the part of that cost attributable to potholes. Next, the team contacted resurfacing companies in the area to get an idea of what covering materials were available and their cost. Once all of this information had been gathered, a presentation to the lead team was made because the project involved a fairly large expenditure. The whole dock could be covered with a rubberized cement compound for approximately $80,000. The most used and heavily pocked corridors could be resurfaced for approximately $6,500. This was an area of approximately 1,600 square feet. During the previous year, $16,000 had been spent replacing tow motor tires alone and $13,000 replacing axles. At least half of this amount was estimated to be excessive.

The lead team immediately okayed resurfacing the most heavily traveled area. However, it asked the sheet finishing team to wait until the purchasing department could check its recommendations concerning materials and suppliers. During this wait the maintenance team developed a more extensive training program for tow motor operators. Three weeks later the team was told to proceed with its plan as presented. The resurfacing company covered the designated area. The maintenance team was not satisfied with the job and asked the company to redo it. The company balked. The maintenance team went back to the lead team for assistance. Mr. Dole made a phone call. The company redid the job, this time under the close supervision of maintenance team representatives.

THE PROCESS CONTINUES TO EVOLVE

As the process itself continued to mature, the issue of facilitator training came up. The corporate approach to quality improvement was to train management, facilitators, and team members before forming teams. The OD section squad had obviously not done that. Rather, it had made training part of more action- and result-oriented activities. The most important objective, in terms of this alternative, was to quickly get employees directly involved in systemic improvement efforts. It was to gain access to and effectively begin utilizing their expertise. It was to generate highly visible improvements based on this expertise, which would help inspire the requisite, overall sense of involvement, ownership, and commitment.

Facilitators and team members had been given, through demonstration, the bare basics in group process and problem-solving skills during the start-up exercise and early sessions. It was assumed that, as they progressed and encountered more sophisticated challenges, the facilitators would identify further process-related needs. The key difference was that the facilitators would be identifying such needs based on their own experience rather than having the needs defined for them.

During this period, the facilitators had formed a team of their own. They planned to meet every other week to share experiences and discuss process issues. While the first facilitators had been somewhat hesitant about accepting this role and taking on another responsibility, Mac now had a list of volunteers from a number of staff departments. The realization had come quickly that the position provided excellent, hands-on training in important management skills. It gave those involved access to more people and areas of the mill than they had previously enjoyed. It gave them direct contact with the manufacturing process and its problems. It allowed them to better understand how their own jobs fit in to the total operation. Finally, when a team was doing well and completing projects, the position gave the young facilitators positive exposure to upper-level management.

The team's first decision was that each facilitator should handle no more than one team. Otherwise, the load of meetings and support activities interfered too greatly with normal job responsibilities. When some facilitators complained about the lack of up-front formal training, it was pointed out that they were producing good results without it. When they wanted more training, however, all they had to do was design the session, and it would be theirs.

An issue brought up by the lead team during this period was how best to alert the rest of the mill work force to team activities. Bulletin boards were hung in each area with notes on the activities released by the teams. The mill communicator began meeting regularly with Mac and sitting in on selected team meetings. He published accounts of the progress of a variety of team projects in the mill newspaper and released special bulletins.

One project that the lead team had been working on was an employee security statement. Eventually, a copy of it was distributed to every member of the work force. The statement said, briefly, that in order for the mill to remain competitive, jobs had to change as technology changed. This, however, did not mean that employees would be laid off. Layoffs hadn't happened as a result of past changes and wouldn't happen in the

Table 8.1
Final List of Ideal Characteristics for the Product Distribution Function

1. Distribution system handled as a business with suppliers and customers.
2. First step a quality inspection/rejection.
3. Minimal handling.
4. Mostly live loading.
5. Few scheduling changes.
6. Centralized control.
7. Computerized control.
8. Computerized control of carrier pool and docking facilities.
9. Tow motor operators needing less supervision.
10. Low-cost carrier used.
11. Trucks loaded from dock closest to paper location.
12. Loading and bracing of trucks and rail cars done according to customer specifications.
13. Minimal reloading.
14. Final inspection/verification.
15. Twenty-four-hour turn-around time for carriers.

future. The mill valued its employees and their expertise and didn't want to lose either. While lifetime employment could not be guaranteed, employees should be assured that management would do everything within its power to retain them.

The distribution of the statement was followed by question-and-answer sessions for each shift during which Mr. Dole himself fielded most of the questions.

The lead team had also finished its idealization of what was now called the "distribution" function. It included input from all critical stakeholders. The mission statement for this function now read, "On-time, nondamaged deliveries of exactly what is ordered by the customer." The list of ideal function characteristics had been expanded (see Table 8.1). Design details had been worked out to bring many of these characteristics to life. Implementation steps were being framed and scheduled.

THE PROCESS JELLS

By this time, the mechanics of the hourly team building effort were fairly sound. Process momentum was building. What remained was to start

Table 8.2
List of Hourly Teams in Completed Quality Improvement Process Network

PS&D

  1. Customer service

  2. Roll finishing

  3. Sheet finishing

  4. Maintenance

Paper

  5. Machines 1 and 2

  6. Machines 3 and 4

  7. Maintenance

Pulp

  8. Operators

  9. Maintenance

Power

  10. Operators

  11. Maintenance

Technical

  12. Operators

  13. Engineers

Administrative

  14. Controllers

  15. Human Resources

General Maintenance

  16. Operators

Woodyard

  17. Operators

  18. Maintenance

the rest of the teams gradually. A and B and C and D roll finishing teams had decided to stop meeting separately and to combine their teams. Power operator and power maintenance teams were brought up during the thirteenth week. Pulp, woodyard, general maintenance, and technical services were scheduled to be organized during the following month. The mill-wide network of 18 hourly teams was almost complete (see Table 8.2).

Table 8.3
Work Order System Issues

---

1. How far should facilitators go in weeding out work orders, especially concerning small issues that can be dealt with by the operators themselves?
2. How much maintenance work can production workers themselves do? (This is a union contract issue.)
3. How can area teams keep track of work orders once they are submitted?
4. How do we overcome the team attitude that if their work orders aren't addressed, a boss will be fired?
5. How do we overcome the foremen's fear that if they don't address team work orders they will be fired?
6. Is whatever comes out of teams automatically valid?
7. How do we prioritize team work orders?
8. How do we know how many are coming from a team?
9. The system is lopsided. One maintenance area ends up doing all the work.
10. Teams and area foremen have to coordinate better.
11. Production supervisors need to weed out duplications.
12. Foremen need the authority to do some maintenance scheduling.
13. A feedback process needs to be put in place so that teams can learn why supervisors say "yes" or "no" to work orders. Ground rule 12 has to be enforced.
14. What happens when teams won't accept a "no" response?
15. There needs to be a better system for getting work orders to production supervisors.
16. There needs to be more quality control in the filling out of work orders so that they are understandable.
17. Teams should be forced to justify work orders. Ground rule 11 has to be enforced.
18. Is a one-week response time to work orders feasible?
19. Will team work orders receive the same or more priority than those already in the system?
20. How many work orders is a team allowed to have in the system at once?

Table 8.4
Improved System for Handling Team-Generated Work Orders

---

1. Work order priorities set by production supervisor based on project merit but with special attention paid to those submitted by hourly teams.

2. Facilitators responsible for educating teams so that they understand how the work order system works, how priorities are set, what the maintenance work load is.

   - Team writes work orders at conclusion of each meeting and puts the team's priority for the project on the work order.
   - Facilitator signs the work order.
   - Facilitator gives work order to production supervisor unless decided otherwise by production supervisor and facilitator.
   - Production supervisor responds to team facilitator on decision concerning work order during week following submission. The response may be: (a) Yes, it's a good idea and scheduled for . . . (b) No, I don't think it's a good idea and here's why . . . or (c) We need to talk about this . . .
   - Facilitator responsible for keeping track of work order status until work is completed to satisfaction of team.
   - If the response to a work order is "no" and the team disagrees with the production supervisor's rationale, the facilitator presents the team's objections to the production supervisor. If the production supervisor continues to disagree, he or she meets personally with the team.

The facilitator team sent a request to corporate quality for training in facilitation skills. Two trainers arrived and were impressed with the level of understanding that the mill facilitators had already achieved. One of them stayed to become more familiar with the team building process.

Not all of the teams were doing well. Some had difficulty getting members to follow through on action steps. Some had trouble getting members to attend, especially when they were off shift. A pattern was eventually discernible. Each team developed a hard core of four or five members who attended most of the meetings and did most of the work on projects. Others came and went in cycles. A team would be well attended and extremely active for several months, then would hit a lull, then would revitalize itself, usually around a new project. While the ground rule concerning attendance was necessary to set the tone, it was obviously not enforceable. The process had to sell itself to employees, which, in general, it was doing.

The second-level teams continued to present problems. Though three were in place and working on projects, their value remained questionable.

Supervisors were complaining about the amount of time that hourly representatives to these teams were away from their jobs. A consulting firm, MTT, was simultaneously leading a mill-wide technical training effort, so that shifts were being further depleted. The OD consultants argued that the team building effort should take precedence over the MTT effort. Technical training would be more valuable when the workers themselves defined the need for it. The MTT consultants, of course, had a different perspective.

Supervisors and foremen had other ongoing concerns about the process. One continued to be the work order system. They remained dissatisfied with the way that team-generated work orders were being handled. Representatives of the supervisors and foremen eventually met with the facilitators and drew up a list of issues (see Table 8.3). When this list had been completed, the combined group designed an approach to handling team-generated work orders that was acceptable to all (see Table 8.4).

CHAPTER 9

Finishing Up

KEY BUILDING BLOCKS

Once all the hourly teams were in place, the OD consultants sat down with Mr. Dole, the manager of human resources, and Mac to evaluate their progress thus far and to define future steps. Several key issues were discussed. These included:

1. The fact that Mac had rapidly become overloaded. Keeping tabs on 18 hourly teams and taking the lead in resolving process and logistical issues, as well as continuing to meet his normal responsibilities, was too much for one person to manage effectively.

2. Middle management's continuing lack of support. A meeting had been held to discuss the concerns of these men and women. Some wanted to reorganize the teams according to shifts to cut down on overtime. Some wanted maintenance representatives assigned permanently to the production teams. Some wanted supervisors to sit on hourly teams and to define the projects that these teams would work on. Few were satisfied with the current situation.

3. The third was a process issue that contributed to the second. The second-level teams were still not functioning well. This was due partially to ongoing confusion about what these teams should be

working on. It also resulted from a lack of support by supervisors supposed to participate. The third-level team had met only twice, then had gone out of existence. No one saw a need to revive it in light of the guarantees provided by the ground rules and the effectiveness of task forces. People were saying the same thing about the second-level teams.

4. A continuing lack of adequate recognition for all that had been accomplished by teams. Hourly workers wondered if the corporation actually knew or cared about the improvements they had made.

Two decisions came out of this review session. The first concerned process facilitators. Some of the most experienced ones were to be given the added title of "area coordinator." Their new responsibilities would include trouble-shooting and coordinating the efforts of all the teams in one area—for example, PS&D, paper, or pulp. This arrangement would take some of the load off Mac while at the same time giving the veteran facilitators a new challenge.

It was also decided that the facilitator network should idealize its own operation. It should define its mission, identify desirable network characteristics, then redesign the facilitating system entirely if need be. The exercise would include a review of the ground rules first introduced by the OD consultants. Perhaps, based on experience, these too would need revision.

It was obvious that the facilitator network was now ready to assume process ownership, which had been an OD team objective from the start. The idealization exercise was an excellent vehicle for encouraging the involved transfer. It began immediately and was met with a good deal of enthusiasm.

The second decision to come out of the review session concerned middle managers. Most superintendents, supervisors, and foremen felt that they had been victimized by the process. Foremen and supervisors had been forced to watch their traditional powers erode as hourly workers, with the support of top management, took on more responsibility and authority.

Also, corporate was again encouraging the mills to dissolve management layers in order to improve communication. In response to this encouragement, as well as to the functional breakdown upon which the team building process was based, Mr. Dole had decided to redefine his management team's role. Foremen were to take over full responsibility for the actual manufacturing process in their areas. Supervisors were to be renamed "project supervisors" and were now responsible for *improving* manufacturing systems rather than running them. Both foremen and supervisors would report directly to the division superintendent.

The supervisors did not understand their new role. They felt that they were being shoved aside. Their scapegoat was the team building process, which they said had precipitated all these unwelcome changes.

It was obvious to everyone that a way now had to be found to involve supervisors more fully and to gain their commitment to the process—a way that clarified their new responsibilities and made these acceptable but that did not allow them to take control of the hourly teams.

The OD consultants met with the lead team to discuss the best way of bringing the supervisors on board. It was suggested that a network of design teams be started at this point to complement the hourly problem-solving teams. The design teams should be composed mainly of supervisors. Someone asked what the difference between problems and design projects was. The OD consultants answered that while problem-solving teams worked, at least initially, on smaller, isolated changes—safety repairs, manufacturing process adjustments, equipment purchases, and environmental improvements such as the installation of fans—design team efforts would be broader in scope and would focus on entire systems, such as the shift system, the roll rejection system, and the purchasing system. In their new role as system "improvers," supervisors were the ideal leaders for such projects because of their years of hands-on experience and their breadth of perspective.

It was suggested that the lead team members should break down their areas of responsibility into key systems, then identify those that could stand improvement and assign a team of area supervisors to work on each.

One of the managers broke in to say that if hourly problem-solving team members were considered mature enough to pick their own projects, he thought that supervisors should be, too. The rest of the group agreed. The lead team eventually decided to start a design team to represent each major functional area, to see what projects the teams came up with, and then, if necessary, to reorganize the team network to deal more effectively with the number and types of projects.

DESIGN TEAMS TAKE THE LEAD

During the following two months, 23 design teams composed of supervisors were formed across the mill to complement the 18 hourly problem-solving teams that had resulted from a merger. The design teams were facilitated by former problem-solving team facilitators chosen by Mac.

Table 9.1
Pulp Area Design Team Start-up Exercise Results

---

1. External Stakeholders

Paper Mill	Power House (WTP)
Woodyard	Evaporators (Hot Water)
Caustic Plant	Railroad
Bleach Plant	Truckers (Suppliers)
Engineering (Process)	Environmental Services (Clarifier-Reclaimer)
Unions	Purchasing
Administrative Services	

2. Key Technical Systems

Digester	Liquor Recovery
Chip Silo	Storage
Wet Room	Testing
Warm Water System	Instrumentation
Turpentine	Communications
Condensate	

3. Key Management Systems

QIP	Shift System
Union	Motivation
MTS	Communications
Safety	

4. System Most in Need of Improvement Is Digester. Important Questions Concerning It Include:

1. What causes it to hammer (TC vibration)?
2. Why are P numbers so erratic?
3. What causes internal scale build-up?
4. Concerning daily production
   - How much are we making?
   - How much should we make?
   - What is it designed to make?
5. How should it be controlled?
6. Why can't variables be consistently measured?
7. Why can't we have good standard chips?
8. Why can't we get maintenance process training?
9. Why not buy chips?

Table 9.1 *(continued)*

5. Characteristics Digester System Should Ideally Include:

1. Uniform chips
2. Uniform liquor
3. Good level control
4. Wash liquor quality
5. Temperature control for steam
6. Design capacity greater than daily needs
7. Do continual training without overtime
8. Have skilled experienced digester operators
9. Good communication with process suppliers (liquor, chips, etc.)
10. Train engineering with maintenance and operators

6. Actions Steps to Be Completed Before Next Meeting

1. Check with Hammermill process groups for their method of measuring white liquor.
2. Check with woodyard to use #5 silo as "own-made" chip silo. This was done before but is no longer standard operating procedure.

New recruits took over the problem-solving teams. The start-up took one and a half hours, instead of three hours as with the problem-solving teams. An explanation of the team building process and its objectives was no longer necessary. Everyone was familiar with it by this time. The time usually spent up front building a relationship between the consultants and new team members was also eliminated.

For each area represented, the OD consultants had design team members identify: key stakeholders for that area; technical systems important to the area operation when a line unit was involved; administrative procedures important to the area operation when a staff unit was involved; and key management systems that impacted the area's productivity. Teams then picked the technical system, administrative procedure, or management system that they thought needed the most improvement. They generated a list of questions that they wanted to ask concerning that system/procedure. They developed a list of characteristics that the system/procedure should have ideally. They then began defining action steps necessary either to discover the answer to their questions or to redesign system/procedure parts so that they took on the desired characteristic. Finally, they identified stakeholders whose input was required before changes were implemented and discussed the design with them. The results of the start-up exercise for the pulp operation team can be found in Table 9.1.

The initial projects embarked on by these teams included the redesign of the standard cost system, the wood handling system, the stock prep system, the mail system, the roll wrapping system, the bleaching system, the internal communication system, the digester system, the steam allocation system, and the time reporting system.

BEST ROLE FOR THE LEAD TEAM

The lead team had completed its idealized design of the PS&D function. Lead team QIP sessions had eventually been combined with morning production meetings. Quality process issues, however, had not fared well against operational issues in the ensuing competition for time. It was decided, therefore, to reintroduce a weekly lead team session dedicated solely to QIP-related activities.

Now that supervisor teams were redesigning departmental systems on a mill-wide basis, the lead team opted to work on three critical macro-level issues that affected everyone. The first was the mill's relationship with outside stakeholders such as Woodlands and the corporate customer service staff. The team felt that several of these relationships needed realignment.

The second issue was training. The corporation had made major changes in its training program over the last several years. Not all of them had been acceptable to employees for a variety of reasons. Several hourly teams had already attempted to deal with local training issues, but their efforts had been piecemeal. The lead team decided to develop a comprehensive and realistic model of its own for employee training that would incorporate the technical training still being carried out by the MTT consulting group and the training in statistical process and quality control for which they felt the work force was now ready.

The third issue involved discovering ways to increase operational effectiveness. The lead team decided to explore the possibility of turning key mill areas—the woodyard, pulp, paper, power, PS&D, maintenance, and so on—into a continuum of profit centers. The controller first had to come up with a system for estimating costs and profits, then define what needed to be measured. After this, the engineers needed to develop standards and a means of measurement.

Two lead team members were given responsibility for developing projects around each of these issues. The team also defined its own "miniset" of ground rules to govern its output. These were:

1. Everyone affected must have the opportunity for input.
2. Designs must be technologically feasible and financially appropriate.
3. Results must promote an ethical business philosophy.
4. Results must promote employee security.

As time passed, however, very little happened. Lead team meetings were enthusiastic. Everyone continued to participate. Yet action steps were not completed and the projects eventually bogged down. It became obvious that asking managers at this level to work on projects outside team meeting hours was an unwise move. Too much was going on operationally. The mill was preparing for union contract negotiations. Also, another major shake-up was occurring at corporate headquarters.

At that point, Ed suggested that the lead team's focus be shifted away from design issues and concentrated, at least in the short term, on its third responsibility—reviewing, contributing to, and helping coordinate the efforts of supervisor and hourly teams. Such a shift would relieve lead team members of unwanted outside work and, at the same time, increase the team's visibility.

THE FACILITATOR EXERCISE

The facilitator network had, by this time, designed its ideal self. Its mission was "to help the Eastern Mill be the best by managing the development and implementation of improvements originated by QIP teams." The ideal systems characteristics defined as necessary to the realization of this mission were:

1. Management support
2. Adequate training
3. Dedicated facilitators
4. Career advantages
5. Good understanding/support from middle management
6. Good communication among facilitators
7. Well-defined goals
8. An apprenticeship program for facilitator trainees
9. The ability to coordinate hourly- with management-level goals

The facilitators began working on the actualization of the second characteristic—adequate training. They defined the types of training desired, then began exploring sources. Within two weeks a course in problem-solving technique had been scheduled for all facilitators. Those who had not yet taken the corporate leadership/communications skills course were signed up to do so. A new, refresher course in this same area was being designed. A system to circulate relevant articles through the facilitator network was being put into place. Finally, the group was developing an apprenticeship program for newly recruited facilitators.

By this time the team network was complete and running smoothly. Mac and his lead facilitators (area coordinators) were making process decisions. The OD consultants were simply advising. The corporate CEO had stated in a recent speech that people who wanted to stay with and progress in Core Corporation must actively support QIP. This sentiment was repeated by Mr. Dole to his supervisors, a diminishing number of whom were still resisting the change in their role.

During the OD consultants' ongoing conversations with middle managers, most of them said that they were willing to push decision-making authority down into the hourly ranks, but that when something went wrong, they were the ones who got blamed, so they were afraid to take the risk. This issue was brought to the lead team's attention. Its members decided that more stress should be put on the positive. Employees shouldn't be afraid to make mistakes when they were trying hard, so long as they learned from them. A differentiation was made by one lead team member between honest mistakes and those caused by not caring, by sloppiness. Too many of the latter type were still occurring. It was pointed out by another member that when the process was working properly, peer pressure became the main form of "punishment" for goofing off rather than a bawling out by the boss.

Another issue brought up at the lead team meeting was that several of the design teams were having difficulty understanding whether their assignment was to redesign entire areas at once or whether they could focus incrementally on the systems within their areas. The lead team eventually decided to leave this decision up to the design teams. They could begin with increments. As more and more pieces of the puzzle were completed and had to be fit together, however, the need for an overall area design would become apparent on its own.

FACILITATOR TRAINING

The facilitators held their first home-grown workshop on two consecutive days over lunch. Lead team members were invited. The sessions were well attended. Thirty-one facilitators came the first day, and 33 the second. There was now a total of 41 facilitators. Those who missed were on vacation, taking courses, or in foreman slots where they couldn't leave the floor.

The workshop was built around the following agenda:

Day One

1. Review and discussion of ground rules, which facilitators had revised to better fit the mill's situation (see Table 9.2).

2. Review and discussion of the facilitator's role (see Table 9.3).

Table 9.2
Eastern Mill Facilitators' Revised Version of Process Ground Rules

1. All team members are equal.
2. All team discussions/minutes are confidential unless released by team.
3. One-week response time allowed on feedback, i.e., yes or no status.
4. All "no" responses must be accompanied by an explanation.
5. Teams have access to all mill personnel for informational needs.
6. Teams are accountable for identifying alternates for:
    *   vacations
    *   absenteeism
    *   replacements
7. Department heads/supervisors must be notified of team replacements.
8. Teams elect their own representatives for participation on higher-level teams. At the second level, representation cannot be by foremen solely.
9. Improvements/changes that go outside your "25 square feet" must involve those affected.
10. The transformation system is not intended to replace operating systems, i.e., the work order system, requisition system, approval system.
11. All team-identified problems must be accompanied by a recommended solution and justification. This is a must!
12. Teams will meet on a regularly scheduled basis.
13. All improvements/changes agreed upon at the appropriate level within the team system must follow the approval process of the operating system.
14. When a ground rule is violated, the affected team facilitator will meet with violators for resolution. If the problem is not overcome, the facilitator will report the violation to the lead facilitator. If further action is necessary, the lead facilitator will take it to the lead team.

Table 9.3
Facilitator's Roles

---

1. *Coordinator* **of Pre- and Post-Meeting Logistics**

   - Agenda
   - Minutes
   - Resources
   - Time
   - Location

2. *Team Trainer*

   - Ground Rules
   - Problem-Solving Techniques
   - Work Order Process
   - Patience
   - Presentation Skills

3. *Referee*

   - Between Team Members
   - Between Team Members and Outside Stakeholders
   - Between Team Members and Outside Trainers

4. *Coach* **to Provide**

   - Focus
   - Guidance
   - Motivation

5. *Protector* **of**

   - Individuals
   - Ideas
   - Company Interests
   - Resources

6. *Equalizer* **to Keep Balance of**

   - Participation
   - Projects
   - Business/Socializing

7. *Cheerleader* **to Provide**

   - Praise
   - Encouragement
   - Active Support

Table 9.3 *(continued)*

8. *Press Agent* **to Insure Team Gets**

   • Recognition

9. *Interrogator* **to Perhaps Most Importantly**

   • Ask Questions!

---

3. Skit portraying a "typical" team meeting, with senior facilitators demonstrating some of the problems that arise and how they might be handled.
4. Participants divide into teams, work on prepared situations, present results, and discuss alternatives.
5. Participants review and clarify steps in team design exercise.

Day Two

Conversation with the lead team representatives. Questions addressed included:

1. Does a team have any recourse if it doesn't agree with a supervisor's rejection of a team solution to a problem addressed?
2. What kind of involvement/direction can design teams expect from the lead team?
3. How much time should be spent during work hours on facilitation of QIP team projects?
4. What is the priority of QIP items versus day-to-day items?
5. Is a seven-day response time feasible? If so, how can the lead team help encourage the required response?

One of the remaining process issues was recognition. A need existed to encourage increased "applause" for individual team accomplishments on a mill-wide basis. Several steps were taken. The first was to compile a record of the more than 250 projects completed by teams thus far. A booklet containing this record was printed and distributed so that employees could begin to gain some idea of the big picture, of what had been happening in parts of the mill other than their own, of the breadth and volume of activity. A second step was to videotape some of the most rewarding projects for distribution inside the mill and throughout the corporation.

Figure 9.1
Latest Composition of Eastern Mill Team Network

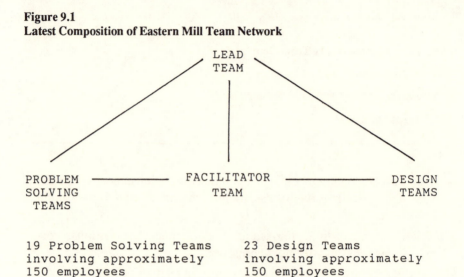

19 Problem Solving Teams
involving approximately
150 employees

23 Design Teams
involving approximately
150 employees

By the end of 1985 the Eastern Mill had set yearly records in 20 major categories, most of them production. Mr. Dole was eventually named "Mill Manager of the Year." The OD consultants stopped traveling to the mill on a regular basis. They were again on call, leaving it up to Mac and Mr. Dole to decide when and if they should come down. Mac called in approximately every other week for several months, then monthly to discuss what was going on. The team network had become a simple but effective two-layer system with the lead team on the top level and the hourly problem-solving teams, almost all of which now included one or two foremen, and the supervisor design teams, most of which now included foremen and superintendents, below (see Figure 9.1).

CHAPTER 10

A Different Situation

THE STRIKE

Approximately a year later, the OD team was asked to give a presentation of its approach to quality improvement at Core's Western Mill. Ed and Gail were on other assignments, so Tom was sent alone. This mill, another one of the largest in the system, housed five paper machines. Approximately 1,000 hourly and 175 salaried employees ran the operation. The mill produced a wide range of paper products, as well as flash-dried and raw pulp.

Due at least partially to the diversity of operations, the mill had for a long while not generated the profits it was capable of producing. Another reason for its subpar performance was a history of strained management-union relations. An increasingly adversarial stance had been developing until, when Tom arrived, a strike was a serious possibility, if not a probability.

The Western Mill differed from the Eastern Mill in that it had a quality improvement department headed by a manager, Sue Lane, who reported directly to the mill manager. The Western Mill had been involved in efforts to improve product quality for several years now. Most recently, an attempt to introduce statistical quality control (SQC) techniques had been made. It had failed due to the inability to foster the necessary level of employee commitment. Also, earlier, a large number of quality circles had been formed. This tactic had also foundered, due mainly to a lack of necessary integration.

Tom spoke to a gathering of the manager's direct reports, outlining the systemic approach, including the team building paradigm and the logic behind it, introduced at the Eastern Mill. After questions were answered, the managers voted to proceed. However, despite Tom's argument that the process would help improve management-labor relations and provide alternatives to a strike, they also decided to wait until after the union contract had been negotiated to begin.

Soon thereafter, two of the three mill unions, the United Paperworkers International Union (UPIU) and the International Brotherhood of Firemen and Oilers (IBFO) rejected the contract offered by the company and struck. The office workers union did not. The corporation, in reaction, began almost immediately replacing the strikers. Most of these new people had no background in pulp or paper making. The situation was made worse by the fact that quite a bit of damage had been done by the departing strikers.

TIME TO GET GOING

Several months later, when it had become obvious that the strikers were not going to win, Tom was asked to return to the mill and start the team building effort. Everyone there was tired. Twelve- and 16-hour shifts were not uncommon. Although the managers were no longer on the floor running the machines, as they had been since the early days of the strike, the mill was still deeply involved in crisis management. The staff was trying to produce paper, train the new hourly work force, repair the damage left behind, and upgrade process technology all at once. The consulting firm MTT had been brought in to head the mill-wide technical training effort. Another firm, Seeco, was also there trouble-shooting management issues.

Many senior managers were skeptical about beginning a team building effort at this point. Too much was already happening. Also, the new employees hadn't been around long enough to understand the manufacturing processes that they worked with, much less improve them. Tom's counterargument was that this, indeed, was the ideal time to change the management culture. Bad habits hadn't formed yet in the new work force. Management-labor relations were still malleable. The new workers were enthusiastic rather than cynical and were eager to make a positive impression. Tom did not say that management was also vulnerable and uncertain at this point and, therefore, probably more willing to try something new.

It was finally agreed that teams would be formed only in PS&D. If these produced anything of value, the process would be spread throughout the mill. If not, it would be put on hold again.

Taking it as a given that the process would go mill-wide, Sue and Tom broke down the entire operation by function. The optimal number of workers in each functionally defined unit was between 40 and 60, though customer service included only 13 and others had close to 80. During this exercise Sue brought Tom and the Seeco trouble-shooter, Gene Rogers, together to compare notes. They quickly realized how neatly their agendas and skills fit and decided to coordinate efforts closely from that point on. Sue and Gene were also experienced trainers and could therefore fill the dual trouble-shooting/training role at the Western Mill that Gail had filled at Eastern. At a later date, efforts were made to incorporate MTT (technical training) into the coordinated approach. The rationalization was that each consulting group provided an important piece, and that by working together rather than competing for time, space, attention, and bodies, they would all look better and do a better job.

As the process matured, the nature of the five phases necessary to any comprehensive QIP discussed in Chapter 2 became increasingly apparent. At Western, the mill manager, Sue, and Gene were handling most of the familiarization phase. Phase two, emplacement of the integrated team network, was Tom and Sue's job. Gene also contributed to this phase by working with managers who were having trouble accepting change. The technical training part of phase three was being covered by MTT. The management systems training part of phase three was divided between Seeco, Sue, and the small in-house training staff. Training in SQC tools, phase four, was put on hold but would eventually be handled by the corporate quality department staff. Finally, Gene had a background in strategic planning and had already begun preparing the lead team for phase five, the planning exercise. Tom would assist, if Gene decided it necessary.

ALL SYSTEMS GO

The initial team model that Sue and Tom decided to put into place was the one that the Eastern Mill had finally adopted. It included only one layer of hourly teams that stretched across the mill, one design team for the supervisors of each department, and the lead team. Task forces would be formed to handle large projects crossing team boundaries.

An important event occurred at this point. The mill manager, who had brought the process in and supported it, left Western to take a position at corporate headquarters. The new mill manager, Ross Emery, was by reputation a strong advocate of employee involvement. Situational demands, however, consumed most of his time and frequently took him off site so that he was unable to provide the constant and extremely visible support and pressure that Mr. Dole had provided at Eastern. He answered all calls for help and followed all process-related suggestions. But he was simply too new and too busy to function as a major resource.

Sue and Tom turned to the department managers for support. At Western there was one for each major area—PS&D, paper, pulp, power, and maintenance. Fortunately, the manager of PS&D became a strong advocate when the team in his area started producing results almost immediately. Most of the other department managers followed suit but not all. When the decision was made to expand the team network beyond PS&D, serious resistance surfaced immediately in the paper machine area. The department manager there was an old-timer, a hands-on type with tremendous technical knowledge. When a machine breakdown occurred, he appeared, orchestrating the necessary repairs or rolling up his sleeves and making them himself.

Market demands and the corporate reward system continued to place emphasis mainly on the number of rolls, sheets, and so on, produced within a given period of time. Quality remained a secondary consideration in most instances. When a paper machine went down, the objective, therefore, was to patch it up and get it running again as quickly as possible. To stand back and try to teach new workers what to do made no sense to this old-timer. The participative team concept also made little sense. It slowed things down. Eventually, this man took a corporate staff position as a technical consultant.

The new head of paper, though also a good leader with a strong technical background, immediately began delegating authority and encouraging his subordinates to do the same. Despite his heavy schedule, he eventually became an hourly team facilitator himself, as did several members of the lead team, making themselves more accessible and responsive to the work force.

The paper-making operation included a number of different functions. It was suggested that putting all of these functions for one paper machine on the same team would improve communication between them. This was tried but with predictable results. Representatives from the individual functions immediately wanted to address issues unique to their function. It was extremely difficult and often impossible to reach consensus on priorities. The teams ended up undertaking several unrelated projects at the same time.

Eventually, the machine-based teams fragmented and had to be reorganized. The reorganization combined the same function across machines so that team members had common problems and could learn from each other. A problem brought up by representatives from machine 1, for example, might already have been solved by workers using machine 3.

DANGER LURKS

The new employees adapted quickly to the team approach. They were willing to attack just about any problem. Very little was accepted as a given. Yet at the same time, they began using the team as an employee-controlled learning vehicle. Management also came to see the team network as a means of speeding up employee training and as a way to give the work force more authority without losing control.

Also, it was not long before some of the managers began viewing the teams as a vehicle for addressing their own priorities. Because these priorities were often critical to the survival of the mill, it was difficult for Sue and lead team members to explain that:

1. The major purpose of the team building effort was to foster commitment to improved quality and that commitment came from a sense of ownership. If managers started dictating team projects, it would be business as usual. During their one-hour meeting per week, the teams should have complete control over what they worked on, bound only by the ground rules.
2. The teams usually picked projects important to the managers anyway. The difference was that they were doing the picking.
3. Managers could form a task force at any time to address a project. They could enlist any employees they wanted for such a task force.
4. Supervisors, at least, would have QIP teams of their own to which they could bring such projects.

Due to the pressures of reorganizing the mill operation, some of the managers had trouble accepting this rationale and continued their efforts to take over the teams. Eventually, Mr. Emery had to intercede and make it absolutely clear that managers could not tell QIP teams what projects to pursue.

LOGISTICS

Tom immediately trained Sue to lead the start-up exercise for both problem-solving and design teams. After several months, Sue was given an assistant who was also trained. Most team meetings were held in a row of classrooms on a balcony above the PS&D area. The team accomplishment posters were hung in the hallway connecting the office building through which most employees entered the mill and the mill proper.

In comparison with the Eastern Mill effort, the lead team's self-defined process-related responsibilities were broader. They included:

1. Developing an overall framework of mill objectives for mill teams into which to fit their projects.
2. Identifying mill-wide issues for the lead team or task forces to pursue.
3. Contributing as a stakeholder to any problem-solving or design team project that involved changes in policy or large expenditures.
4. Setting the example. Helping overcome the reluctance of middle managers by giving them more decision-making authority in their areas of expertise.
5. Being available to all teams as a resource.
6. Functioning as a "reward" to teams by listening to select, short presentations on outside projects as defined and scheduled by the head facilitator.

While discussing point 4, the lead team asked for a clear definition of supervisory responsibility concerning the hourly teams. Sue and Tom drew up a list of "dos" and "do nots" as a guide. The "dos" not covered by the ground rules included:

1. Supervisors do show positive interest in the team's activities. They support team efforts to learn more about departmental systems and to improve them.
2. Supervisors do exercise patience. They realize that this is a learning process for team members and offer their insights and expertise in a nonhostile, encouraging manner.
3. Supervisors do respect team-defined priorities.
4. Supervisors do make team members responsible for implementing approved team-generated changes.

The "do nots" included:

1. Supervisors do not tell teams what projects they can, cannot, or should pursue.

2. Supervisors do not say "no" to or block a team project because they don't believe the team has the right or the expertise necessary to address the involved issue.

3. Supervisors do not punish team members in any way for team-related activities. Problems are brought to the team facilitator, or to the head facilitator if the issue can't be resolved at the team level.

4. Supervisors do not unnecessarily stop team members from attending meetings. We all understand that pulp- and paper-making responsibilities come first. We also know, however, that with adequate planning, it is usually possible to free team members for the required hour or so per week.

5. Supervisors do not "jump" the process by taking over projects that they are interested in or consider to be of great value. Rather, they continue working with the team in order to foster the best alternative along with the desired level of understanding and commitment.

Potential team facilitators volunteered from all areas of the mill. As at Eastern, they were not allowed to facilitate a team representing their own function for fear that they would force their own priorities and improvement-related ideas on the others. As was eventually done at Eastern, "lead" facilitators were also appointed for each department to trouble-shoot the QIP teams in that department, to help integrate team efforts, and to assist in identifying training needs.

The mill manager's secretary took initial responsibility for organizing and feeding the process tracking system. She received copies of all team notes that had been released. She developed two master files, one paper, one computerized. Team folders in the paper file were color coded according to department.

A "team project" form was generated to record monthly progress on larger projects and the results of smaller projects. This form included a space for a cost-benefit analysis and for the recording of actual savings. A copy of the form filled out for each project was placed in both the paper and computerized files.

A "team change notification" form was devised to track changes in team membership. It included a notation on the team meeting time, day, and location. It also included a list of those who were to receive the team's notes.

A "meeting schedule of QIP teams" was developed to consolidate and keep track of the weekly meeting times and locations of all teams. This was published monthly.

A "distribution list" was designed for each department, listing all the teams in the department, their members, their facilitators, and their computer document numbers. Modifications in the team member lists were based on information gleaned from the "team change notification" form.

THE QIP-SAFETY CONNECTION

Another relationship requiring attention at Western was that between the quality improvement effort and the safety record improvement effort. Core, like most modern-day corporations, was extremely safety conscious. The typical safety program includes the following elements:

1. Posters and other educational materials.
2. Presentations on relevant safety issues that act as a reminder of things that employees should already know and as a warning concerning new dangers in the workplace.
3. Periodic crew meetings to pinpoint local safety issues and sometimes to define solutions.
4. Accident reports, monthly records of lost-time and non-lost-time accidents.
5. A head of safety at the facility level responsible for overseeing all of the above.
6. A corporate safety director responsible for coordinating the education program and for reducing accidents on a corporate-wide basis.

Problems with the typical safety program include the following:

1. Lack of ownership by those most important to the program's success.
2. Absence of an appropriate "vehicle" for instituting safety-related changes in the workplace.
3. Dependence on an incentive system that can actually hamper efforts to make the workplace safer.

Concerning the ownership issue, while employees and employee safety committees identify problems, it is usually left up to management to define and to implement the necessary changes. Employees, therefore, do not make the contribution they are capable of making. Members of the work force would be more likely to stress safety if given the power to implement changes that they thought necessary or wise themselves.

This approach makes sense for the following reasons. First, workers know better than managers in most situations what the safety problems are, because they must deal with them on a continuing basis. They also know, for the same reason, what the most appropriate solutions are. Second, because there are more workers than managers, if given the necessary authority and access to resources, the workers can deal with more problems in a shorter period of time. Third, foremen and other managers usually have a greater number of responsibilities than workers, with safety-related improvements being just one. They also frequently have a different set of priorities, so that safety issues important to workers take a back seat. When workers have ownership, a number of steps in the correction process are eliminated, and constant monitoring and proper feedback are better assured. As a result of this last advantage, the chances for communication foul-ups and for a work order to get lost or buried, for example, are reduced.

In terms of an effective change vehicle, very few corporations have put into place that which is necessary. What generally occurs is that projects compete for attention on all levels. Individual employees or small groups bring safety issues to foremen or supervisors. Foremen and supervisors bring their competing lists to the maintenance department. Maintenance combines these lists with lists from other sources and tries to decide which projects to schedule first. Those involving a production process break-down and those submitted by top-level management are generally given priority. Safety projects, unless a crisis or lost-time accident is involved, frequently have to wait.

KEEPING IT LEGITIMATE

In terms of incentives, traditional emphasis has been on reducing the number of accidents, the key word here being "number." As a result of this approach, the corporate-level safety director is graded on how effective he or she is at cutting the number of accidents reported, the key word here being "reported." Such reductions occur in three ways: through luck, through legitimate education efforts, or through illegitimate maneuvering.

"Illegitimate maneuvering" involves finding some way to misrepresent reality. One means of doing this is by simply fudging the figures. An extreme example would be to not consider an accident reportable unless the victim is carried out on a stretcher. Another less extreme example would be to give an employee with a banged-up leg the job of monitoring the infirmary waiting-room television screen until he or she can return to normal duties so that no lost time need be reported.

A second, more subtle strategy is for the corporate safety director to let it be known that accident rates are expected to decrease and that managers' careers could be adversely affected if they do not. As a result, workers are forced to begin stocking their lockers with medical supplies. If an injury is too serious to deal with in the locker room, an excuse if found to go home early or to go to a hospital, with coworkers covering the absence.

A third approach is to hassle the workers who do bring their injuries to the infirmary, to make them fill out long accident reports, to investigate the accident in order to discover the degree of negligence involved, and to broadcast the injured worker's name along with an account of the "crime."

In terms of the existing incentive system, the point is that as a result of management's current emphasis on numbers and on racking up a record total of accident-free days—a quantitative rather than a qualitative thrust—safety programs frequently end up alienating the very people whose quality of working life and productivity they are being run to improve. Employees become the victims rather than the beneficiaries of the involved efforts.

There are several ways to make safety programs more effective. Perhaps most important, top-level management should stop broadcasting the numbers, at least at the corporate level. This practice puts emphasis in the wrong place. It turns safety into a competitive rather than a cooperative effort. It places unrealistic demands on the corporate-level safety program director, which can warp his or her perspective and cause that person, in turn, to place unrealistic demands on unit safety heads.

The corporate director's role should be threefold. First, that person should function as a resource. The director should make sure that all units know about and have access to training materials. Second, that person should facilitate the organization and integration of training efforts throughout the company. Third, the director should make sure that top-level management is kept abreast of developments and that it continues to demonstrate highly visible support for the effort.

The head of safety at the unit level should again act as an organizer and integrator for safety improvement efforts. This person should make sure that an appropriate change vehicle exists and that employees have access to all useful resources. This person should also be in charge of mounting an effort to encourage employees to seek help at the infirmary when injured and should strive to make the involved process as painless as possible. The espoused theory should be that workers don't want to get hurt, and that when they do get hurt the company wants to help rather than embarrass them. Records of the number and types of accidents that occur at the unit level should be used to pinpoint trouble areas in the operation rather than to judge individual performance.

Safety, in effect, should no longer be something "done" to workers or taught to them by management. Rather, the workers should teach, oversee, and insure safety for themselves. It should become part of their everyday activities, their self-defined job responsibilities.

Safety and quality improvement are inseparable. When employees are given responsibility for improving the quality of manufacturing processes and the work environment, safety is, almost without exception, their first consideration. At Western, due to the new unskilled work force, the number of repairs and modifications being made, and the fact that the striking unions had lodged a number of complaints with OSHA that precipitated a formal inquiry, it was a necessity as well as a consideration. A new director of safety joined the human resources department staff at the same time that Tom began working with Sue, and she eventually launched a safety education and improvement effort complete with area teams. This was unfortunate because at least 40 percent of the initial improvements made by the hourly QIP teams were safety related and were already addressing many of the issues her teams would address.

Sue suggested as an alternative that the safety director focus on education; that task forces governed by the same ground rules as the QIP teams be formed around specific safety projects identified by the lead team and others; and that, rather than forming her own teams, the safety director help facilitate and integrate safety-oriented projects generated by the QIP teams.

CHAPTER 11

Critical Mass Is Achieved

RESTRUCTURING THE MILL
MANAGEMENT SYSTEM

As process trouble-shooter, Gene Rogers had been meeting with both groups and individuals to try to help them understand and accept their role as it was being redefined by the QIP. During one of these sessions with the mill's area supervisors, participants began identifying systems improvements specific to their level that they wanted to address. Gene, and Sue, who was working with him, suggested that the group turn itself into a QIP team representing a level of management, rather than a function, and join the QIP team network.

During the start-up exercise, the area supervisors' number-one priority quickly became obvious. They wanted a clear definition of their responsibilities. It also became clear that they wanted the departmental managers, their bosses, to step aside and let them run the day-to-day operations. Finally, it became clear that they saw little possibility of this occurring. The old ways of doing things were too firmly entrenched.

They were eventually convinced to participate in the design of what they considered to be the ideal situation. Early team meetings were poorly attended. A hard core of approximately 10 supervisors always showed up and did most of the initial work. As the design began to evolve and make

Table 11.1
Area Operations Team Composition for Groundwood

Core Members

1	Area Supervisor
1	Shift Supervisor
1	Operator
1	Maintenance Foreman
1	Maintenance Analyst
1	Equipment Reliability Foreman
1	Preventive Maintenance Manager
1	I and E Maintenance Representative
1	Project Engineer (Department)
1	Training Coordinator (if existing)

10

Consultants

1	IR Representative
1	Engineering Representative
1	Finance Representative
1	Purchasing Representative
1	Safety Representative

5

---

sense, however, enthusiasm built. Eventually, 20 or more supervisors began attending.

Within two months, the team had designed an ideal management system strawman. The design that team members created began with an operations "coordinating team" on which were area supervisors representing every department. The coordinating team met every morning to share information, to discuss the previous day's operation, and to coordinate that day's planned activities.

The coordinating team was to be fed by 13 "area operations teams," one for each key production function. These would be composed of: all area supervisors working in that function; representatives from other levels of that function; and representatives from other functions affecting that function.

Membership of the 13 area operations teams was to be broken down into "core members" and "consultants." The core members would attend on a regular basis. The consultants would attend on an as-needed basis. The composition of the groundwood area operations team can be found in Table 11.1.

The area operations teams were to take charge of planning and overseeing the daily manufacturing operation. The issues that they planned to accept primary responsibility for included:

1. Quality
2. Safety
3. Production Levels
4. Environment
5. Requirements Concerning Hourly Employees
6. Costs
7. Production Planning
8. Maintenance Planning
9. Morale
10. Training
11. Scheduling

Finally, a representative of the coordinating team would regularly attend lead team meetings to report its activities and gain input from lead team members.

Instead of overseeing day-to-day operations, the lead team's new primary role in this scenario would be to develop long-term mill objectives on which the coordinating team could base its activities. In turn, the lead team would be required to incorporate into its plan priorities defined by the coordinating team and the area operations teams.

Several lead team members became deeply concerned about this project, suggesting that it exceeded the charter of the QIP. An attempt was even made at one point to force the area supervisors to drop it and turn their attention to safety issues. Sue and Tom went to the mill manager and explained the situation. He responded immediately by attending an area supervisors' team meeting and voicing his support for this particular project.

Eventually, four of the most active members of the area supervisors' team presented the preliminary design to the lead team for its input as a major stakeholder. During this exchange, most of the confusion and misinformation that had led to the opposition was cleared up.

Next, the area supervisors' team began working on project action steps. These included:

1. Put formation of the coordinating team on hold until area operations teams are in place.

2. Work on developing one or two area operations teams. Get them in place and functioning properly before forming any more.

3. Develop area operations teams in areas that already have hourly problem-solving and supervisory design teams in place.

4. Have the department manager and area supervisors identify the area operations team's core members and consultants.

5. Familiarize members of an area operations team with that area's overall operation.

6. Familiarize all employees in each area with the area operations team's role and responsibilities.

7. Experiment with how often area operations teams should meet, when, and where.

While some of the area operations teams started functioning almost immediately, it soon became obvious that getting all 13 in place would take a long time. The area supervisors, therefore, decided to go ahead and form the coordinating team. Very quickly the work of this group gained the blessing of the entire lead team. Lead team members were relieved of day-to-day issues that had consumed a great deal of their time.

The lead team eventually began meeting only three times a week and was able to focus on strategic issues during these sessions. At the same time, however, lead team members remained fully informed on coordinating team activities and decisions and retained the right to intercede when they thought it necessary. The mill management system that evolved as a result of this project is outlined in Figure 11.1.

RECOGNITION

The area supervisors' team's success gave the overall process a substantial boost. By the latter part of the year, the targeted "critical mass" of support definitely had been generated. The process had taken on its own momentum. Sue and the facilitators possessed the understanding and skills necessary to keep it on track. Enough successful projects, over 150 by this time, had been produced by teams to convert most critics into believers and to move the rest to silence.

Recognition became an important issue. Employees were wondering if anyone was really noticing the improvements that they were making. The facilitators brainstormed this issue and developed a list of possible awards, including:

Figure 11.1
Mill Management System Defined by Area Supervisors' Team

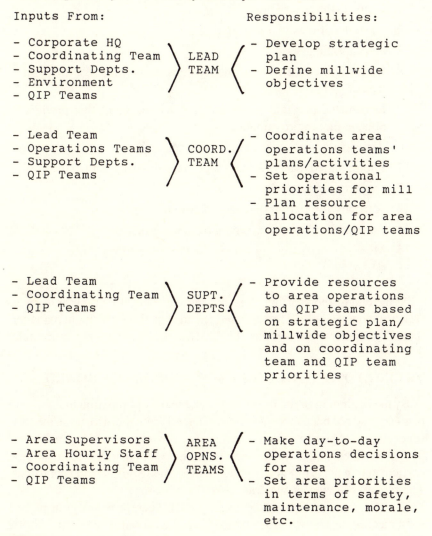

```
Inputs From:                        Responsibilities:

- Corporate HQ                    ⟍           - Develop strategic
- Coordinating Team   LEAD   ⟍  /  plan
- Support Depts.      TEAM   ⟋  \  - Define millwide
- Environment                   /     objectives
- QIP Teams

- Lead Team                       ⟍  /  - Coordinate area
- Operations Teams    COORD. ⟋     operations teams'
- Support Depts.      TEAM   ⟋  \     plans/activities
- QIP Teams                 ⟋      \  - Set operational
                                         priorities for mill
                                      - Plan resource
                                         allocation for area
                                         operations/QIP teams

- Lead Team                       ⟍  /  - Provide resources
- Coordinating Team   SUPT.  ⟋        to area operations
- QIP Teams           DEPTS. ⟋  \     and QIP teams based
                            ⟋      \     on strategic plan/
                                         millwide objectives
                                         and on coordinating
                                         team and QIP team
                                         priorities

- Area Supervisors              ⟍  /  - Make day-to-day
- Area Hourly Staff   AREA        operations decisions
- Coordinating Team   OPNS.  ⟋  \  for area
- QIP Teams           TEAMS ⟋      \  - Set area priorities
                                         in terms of safety,
                                         maintenance, morale,
                                         etc.
```

1. Letters of congratulations.
2. Mill manager, department heads, and supervisors visiting team meetings.
3. Letters of commendation added to personnel files.
4. On-floor recognition by supervisors.
5. Team T-shirts.
6. Gestures of personal recognition.
7. Appropriate gifts.
8. Opportunities for work exchange between members of different teams.
9. Designated parking spaces for members of teams that produce outstanding improvements.
10. Articles on projects in the mill newspaper.
11. Photos added to team status sheets on hallway leading to the mill.
12. Project progress bulletin boards.
13. A trophy for team project competition.
14. Luncheons for teams working on same project.
15. Meetings occasionally catered with coffee, doughnuts, and so on.

At the end of the year, when teams started celebrating their anniversaries, a luncheon was held for each and attended by the department manager, the mill manager whenever possible, and Sue and Tom whenever possible.

TRYING TO GET THE SHIFT SUPERVISORS ON BOARD

By the beginning of the following year, the only population that the lead team felt had not been incorporated sufficiently into the effort was the shift supervisors, formerly called foremen. According to reports, a similar problem still existed at the Eastern Mill. Some sat on hourly teams. Some participated in department design team meetings. Some sat on task forces. The majority, however, were not part of any team.

The shift supervisors worked a swing shift. Therefore, any hour picked for a meeting of the whole would exclude at least one-half of that whole. Also, there were too many shift supervisors for one meeting. The chance to participate would be too limited. The decision was made to break down this group by shift, one team per shift, including representatives from across the mill. The shift teams would be encouraged to address level issues, at least initially, as the area supervisor team had, rather than department- or function-specific issues.

The initial sessions, during which the process was described to shift supervisors and potential projects were identified, were well attended. The majority seemed interested in having their own teams and working on their own projects. When the actual team meetings began, however, very few showed up. Many of those who did were shift supervisors already active on hourly or design teams. Others had been encouraged by their bosses to attend. Projects began but were rarely followed through on. Reasons for the lack of attendance included emergencies, scheduling difficulties, and forgetfulness.

Eventually, the teams were disbanded. The mill manager set up, instead, a weekly information session hosted by himself, which all shift supervisors were invited to attend and during which any topic or problem could be discussed. The turnout was relatively good. Another plan was to have the level as a whole develop a list of task-force projects that it thought important. The shift supervisors would then volunteer for teams built around these projects and schedule their own meetings. When one project was completed, those involved could join another ongoing team or develop a new one around a new project. Monthly review meetings would be held to critique progress and to deal with process issues.

THE FINAL PIECE

Within a year and a half, four of the five phases—familiarization, team network emplacement, management and technical systems training, and strategic planning—were in place or being started at Western. The only piece missing was the introduction of statistical techniques as a means of more accurately defining manufacturing-process weaknesses and of calibrating improvements. Some of the teams had already begun inquiring about or devising such techniques on their own to meet project requirements.

Jane Walls, a member of the corporate quality department, had previously worked at Western. She had headed the earlier effort to introduce Deming's statistical quality control package there. She had stayed in close touch with Sue and had followed the progress of the team building and phase integration effort. Jane was therefore the ideal person to provide the technical expertise necessary to the fifth phase.

She met with Sue and Tom, and they mapped out a two-pronged strategy. The first prong involved training facilitators in statistical process control (SPC) techniques so that they could offer this expertise when suitable projects arose. The second prong focused on finding at least one ongoing project in each department and showing how the techniques might be applied in order to improve results. The involved projects did not need to be team generated. In fact, most of them were not.

Attempts were made to get as many young engineers in training and other technical people involved as possible. Again, as with the team building effort, emphasis was on showing employees the power of these techniques by having people learn them through application rather than in the classroom.

END OF THE ROAD

The Western Mill soon began setting production records. By spring Tom had started to play a minor advisory role. The facilitators had begun a critique of the process and a review of the ground rules. They had also brainstormed and come up with an interesting list of possible ways to encourage people to think in terms of quality improvement. This list included:

1. Make bulletin-board displays showing the seven simple tools of SQC.
2. Conduct a poster design competition for the children of employees.
3. Plan tours for employees to see areas upstream and downstream from their own operation to help instill the idea of internal customers and the importance of quality all the way through.
4. Have employees sign personal pledge cards or declarations of quality commitment. Give employees who sign them a momento to maintain awareness, and display their signed cards or declarations in a public place.
5. Conduct a children's essay contest aimed at why quality is important to my country, my community, my parents' jobs, etc.
6. Form a speakers bureau with employees from the community or mill speaking at functions about specific quality topics.
7. Distribute low-cost promotional items to all employees to maintain awareness (hard hat decals, lapel pins, pens, pencils, bumper stickers, etc.).
8. Stuff a quality message into payroll envelopes or print one on checks.

9. Work with information systems to display quality messages on control monitor/desktop screens.
10. Submit a news release on quality improvement efforts to your local newspaper.
11. Host a brown-bag lunch for other local business and industry leaders to share what each is doing to promote quality in their business.
12. Arrange for visits from corporate or plant management to the mill floor as visible evidence of management support for QIP. Have walk-around tours with handshaking, pep talks, employee suggestion sessions, etc.
13. Show or reshow quality related videos ("In Search of Excellence" or some of the Core success stories) at shift change, during lunch hours, or at crew meetings. Many of the elements of these tapes probably have more meaning now that employees have a deeper understanding of quality management than when they were first shown.
14. Set up brown-bag lunches during which employees can talk about QIP in their areas, how it is progressing, success, opportunities, etc. Could be by invitation or open to everyone.
15. Have a quality mascot dress up and make facility tours reminding people of the quality theme and possibly distributing small tokens of awareness.
16. Have employees' children draw pictures of what their parents do at work and display them at the mill (not for judging, just for display). Young children may be supplied with color sheets of facility/product pictures.
17. Encourage children to collect items manufactured by Core and take them to show and tell at school.
18. Invite local governmental bodies/public officials/school administrators to an informal meeting with plant personnel involved in QIP to discuss techniques of quality management being used. Encourage them to use similar techniques to improve the systems in which they are involved.
19. Hang quality month or QIP banner at facility entrance.
20. Send letters from managers to employees recommitting to quality.

Also, the strike had ended. Strikers were now being rehired to fill open positions. A serious effort was mounted to involve them in team activities and to make them understand that the mill was being run in a more participative manner. In most cases, the effort eventually succeeded.

THE EASTERN MILL KEEPS ROLLING

The Eastern Mill's QIP had continued to evolve under Mac's steward-ship. The lead team had decided to form area "business" teams that functioned actually as "division-level" lead teams. These took care of administering the quality-related affairs of the PS&D, paper, pulp, power, and administrative functions. Division managers and superintendents sat on these teams, as did a representative from the engineering department.

Business team responsibilities included: appointing facilitators for teams in their area; defining task-force projects; appointing task-force members; listening to presentations from teams on projects and providing both input and encouragement; and identifying potential projects for teams to work on if they ran out of team-defined projects and chose to work on new ones.

Technical training was continuing with MTT. Other consulting firms were providing management skills training. Statistical quality control training had been introduced and was ongoing.

A SMALL RIPPLE

One other extremely positive interaction with corporate occurred at this point. The manager of business operations for white papers was responsi-ble for planning and coordinating the production of this type of paper by all primary mills. His objective was to satisfy customer needs in the shortest possible time. In order to improve the interaction between the corporate white papers staff and the Western Mill customer service staff, he formed a joint task force. The force's immediate objective was to reduce order cycle time. He adopted the process ground rules used at the Eastern and Western Mills, then asked the OD section staff to assist with an idealization of the system being addressed. The joint mill-headquarters effort was the first of its kind to be set up and run in this manner. It was highly successful, eventually cutting order cycle time almost in half.

CHAPTER 12

Idealizing a Quality Ending

THE CEO TAKES THE LEAD

While the work was continuing at the Eastern and Western Mills, Core Corporation as a whole was not progressing as rapidly as desired. Corporate emphasis remained on the introduction of statistical measurement techniques as the essence of successful quality improvement. The corporate quality department staff were spending a great deal of time on the road evaluating, training, and suggesting improvements. Few manufacturing facilities and few headquarters support units, however, had anything at all comprehensive in place.

The employee assigned to head manufacturing facility efforts was, in most cases, a young engineer or a member of the human resources staff. Rarely had that person received much training, and frequently he or she had other overriding responsibilities.

Quality improvement teams were in place in relatively few instances. Where they were, a scattershot rather than a mill-wide, integrated approach existed. The teams were built around specific projects, or they were hourly teams headed by managers, or they were exclusively management-level teams. In no instance, other than at the Eastern and Western Mills, had all the necessary ground rules been adopted.

At this point in our idealized scenario, Core's CEO decided that it was time to reorganize and reorient the corporate quality improvement process. Several things had become obvious to him. One was that while allowing his facility and corporate support unit managers to go their own ways initially might have been of value in terms of defining possible alternative approaches, it was time to institute one organization-wide model: so that everyone spoke the same language; so that common training themes and generic training modules could eventually be defined; and so that a great deal of the competition could be eliminated and corporate units could contribute meaningfully to one another's efforts.

He had realized that the corporate quality improvement department needed an overhaul. When picking a leader for this department, he concluded that engineering and management skills alone would not suffice. To succeed, the leader would also need to understand quality improvement tools and techniques and to develop a comprehensive quality-related overview encompassing both management and technical systems.

It had become apparent to him that corporate quality department staff could not do everything required themselves. Instead, members should focus first on teaching key people at each facility the necessary familiarization, team building, training, and trouble-shooting skills, then concentrate on facilitating and monitoring their efforts.

The CEO had learned that very few of Core's hourly employees and middle managers were truly committed, that intensive training alone does not generate the necessary attitudinal changes, and that the mills where the current commitment level was highest were those with comprehensive team networks and ground rules in place.

Finally, the CEO had realized that some form of gain sharing was necessary as a long-term incentive. Once employees have developed the necessary sense of commitment and have shown that they can help improve the bottom line on an ongoing basis, they expect and deserve to share in the revenues generated by their additional efforts. Gain sharing is another tangible way for corporate to show its respect and thanks. It is also the best way to insure employee commitment to long-term improvement.

ADJUSTMENTS

With these realizations in mind, the CEO traveled to a number of sites to see exactly what was happening. He had received glowing reports. However, in most instances, these reports turned out to be somewhat exaggerated. Two of the exceptions were the Eastern and Western Mills. The CEO spent two days at each. He sat in on team meetings and training sessions at different levels and became familiar with the ground rules and their significance. He attended a lead team long-range planning session.

On his return to corporate headquarters, the CEO made several announcements. The first was that Rob Dole would become the new head of the corporate quality improvement department. Mr. Dole had the desired engineering and management expertise. He had been with Core for 35 years and was well respected. Finally, he was the senior employee most familiar with the corporate-wide quality improvement approach on which the CEO had decided.

The CEO next announced that because of their contributions to bottom-line improvement, all employees of the Eastern and Western Mills and of two other mills would be granted gain-sharing privileges. Payment would be made in the form of corporate stock. Stock would be paid instead of money to make these employees aware that their ultimate objectives were to improve the performance of the entire corporation rather than just of their individual mills, and to encourage an increasingly cooperative environment.

In line with the above, the CEO announced that bottom-line goals would be set for all other facilities. Upon reaching them, employees at those facilities would also be eligible for the gain-sharing stock program. He said that a formula would be created to allow facilities to share their gain-sharing rewards with corporate support units. The percentage contributed by each facility would be small, but as the number of facilities earning the right to gain sharing grew, so would the stock bonus reaped by corporate staff units. This would encourage the latter to do everything possible to help improve productivity at the mill/facility level.

Next, the CEO announced that the quality improvement department would be made part of human resources. Mr. Dole would technically report to the vice-president of human resources. However, he would also report directly to the CEO. The quality department would offer five types of expertise—familiarization/trouble-shooting, team building, management systems training, SQC/SPC training, and long-range planning. Employees with familiarization, trouble-shooting, management systems training, and SQC/SPC training skills were already quality department members. Sue Lane would be brought in to piece together and head the team building section. Because of her familiarity with the approach being adopted, Jane Walls would take the lead in the SQC/SPC training section.

GETTING IT RIGHT

An organization-wide effort would be mounted to familiarize everyone with the chosen approach. The entire quality improvement department staff would spend a week at either the Eastern or Western Mill learning how the necessary pieces of the vehicle fit together. Afterward, they would develop a presentation. This presentation would initially be delivered to top-level corporate managers during a two-day seminar at one of the mills. Next, it would be delivered to facility and corporate support unit managers who would visit the two mills in shifts so as not to disrupt operations.

The last group to receive the presentation would be the heads of unit quality improvement efforts. Any such people who did not want the responsibility, or had serious trouble accepting the new corporate model, could be replaced with facilitators from the Eastern or Western Mills. Finally, a videotape explaining what had been done at these two mills would be viewed by all middle managers and hourly employees. A question-and-answer session would follow each viewing.

Sue drew her new team building staff from the Eastern and Western Mill facilitator networks. By this time, there were 30 to 40 trained facilitators in each. A good number could be spared without disrupting the process. It was not difficult to find replacements when they left. Sue trained these people in the techniques used to start hourly- and management-level teams. She then sent two of them to one new facility in each division, except the primary mill division, to help build the necessary team network or to reorganize an already existing one.

The facilities picked were those considered furthest along in terms of the newly adopted organization-wide approach and vehicle. They would then be used as models and training grounds for the rest of that division. The main responsibility of Sue's staff at these facilities was, once again, to help groom facilitators.

Sue made a list of the consulting firms that had been used by different mills and the expertise that each offered. There were two groups. The first included firms offering skills not possessed by members of the quality department/human resources staff. These skills included technical training and long-range planning. The second included firms offering skills that the combined quality department/human resources staff possessed.

All eligible consulting firms were introduced to the chosen approach and told that they would have to adapt to it and to cooperate with each other. The second group was also told that it would be responsible for sharing its expertise with in-house team builders, management skill trainers, and trouble-shooters.

A progress chart was started for each facility. When a facility wanted to use an outside consultant from the list, it had to clear its decision with corporate quality. This requirement insured that the proper progression was followed, that, for example, SQC was not introduced before teams were in place and productive. It also helped keep facilities from wasting time with too much unnecessary up-front training. Finally, it allowed the quality department to keep tabs on the effectiveness of consultants and to compare their costs.

After some initial doubts, corporate human resources was extremely pleased with the new arrangement. Human resource departments have always had trouble proving their worth due to their lack of direct impact on the bottom line. Control of the quality improvement effort gives them the desired dollar figures in savings and increased productivity to compare with those flashed by finance, purchasing, production, and so on.

A SECOND WIND

Meanwhile, back at the Eastern and Western Mills, the effort had gained new momentum, due largely to the CEO's announcements. Things had been lagging. The growing competition between facility managers for quality process-related recognition had hampered, rather than improved, communication. For employees, the reward of a better work environment had sufficed for a while but now was getting stale. They had begun looking for more.

The concept of "critical mass" is relevant on both corporate and unit levels. Efforts in individual facilities, no matter how successful, will eventually die if the process does not spread to enough additional facilities that it becomes unstoppable. If a corporate-level critical mass does not materialize, the units with effective efforts in place will become isolated. Pressure to revert to the old ways will grow. A new manager who does not understand the logic and value of what is in place will take over and decide to remodel the effort based on his or her own experience, intuition, and political considerations.

Quality improvement processes, until the very last piece is in place on both the corporate and unit levels, are either expanding and enriching themselves, or dying. There is no stable state. There is no point at which they can simply be maintained without progress. This need for continual expansion is one reason why a systemic perspective is critical.

When Mr. Dole left the Eastern Mill to take over as head of corporate quality, one of his direct reports replaced him, thus insuring process continuity. Another of his direct reports was made manager of a smaller sister mill, putting the key piece in place there, too.

Within three years, a majority of Core's manufacturing facilities and corporate support units had mounted effective quality improvement efforts. Most manufacturing facilities were showing bottom-line improvements. The same basic set of ground rules had been accepted on the corporate level. Any unit, for example, had access to any other unit in the corporation for desired input or decisions. Anyone in Core affected by a unit's decision or project had to be asked for input and had to agree to changes before they were implemented. If a unit was not receiving requested input from another, its head facilitator could appeal to Core's head facilitator, Mr. Dole. If he was also unsuccessful, Mr. Dole could carry the matter to Core's quality process lead team, which included the CEO and all division heads. The lead team met periodically to review process progress, to receive unit presentations, and to participate in the long-range-planning phase by helping spell out corporate objectives.

Units were also encouraged to identify the projects that they wanted to pursue. Corporate, however, was allowed to come up with its own list of suggestions that units could pick from if they desired. Corporate could also form a task force around any project it wished, using anyone that it wanted to.

The most difficult task facing the revamped corporate quality improvement department was developing the necessary communication channels. Billboard displays in the hallway were no longer enough. A centralized computer file into which all units fed projects that they were working on and had completed was created immediately. Whenever hourly, management, or facility teams identified a new project, they were required to check the file, which was also broken down by category, to see if any other unit had started or completed a similar one. If the answer was yes, they were obliged to contact that unit for input, thus potentially saving time while also establishing new communication linkages.

Representatives of all unit facilitator networks met periodically by division to discuss process-related problems and innovations. Representatives of division networks met biannually to do the same.

BALLOONING OUTWARD

Other positive things were happening at both the Eastern and Western Mills. Requests started coming in for presentations on Core's approach to quality improvement, due partially to improvements in product and service quality; due partially to visits made by mill team members to familiarize themselves with the operations and requirements of both suppliers and customers; and due partially to the fact that employees had used the ground rules to seek project and decision input from suppliers and customers who would be affected. When these presentations were made, several of the involved companies asked if Core could supply them with the expertise necessary to start their own process.

The CEO though this a good opportunity and told Rob Dole to organize the effort. Dole decided to do so on a local basis when possible. If the request came from a supplier/customer of the Eastern Mill, for example, that mill would handle the presentation and send personnel to assist. Corporate quality improvement would provide back-up.

At the same time, the Western Mill had followed through on many of the suggestions made during the facilitator brainstorming session. A speaker's bureau made up of employees had been formed to address community groups. Mill personnel began networking with other local companies that had quality improvement efforts in place, and with companies of all sizes interested in starting one. Monthly "brown-bag" lunches were organized so that experiences and ideas could be shared.

Videos were made describing the steps in the mill's process and loaned to anyone in the community who was interested. Open houses were sponsored for local government officials, school administrators, and the heads of nonprofit organizations. The conversation at these open houses centered on how a quality improvement effort similar to the one at the mill might benefit them, and how Core might assist. Eventually, Core helped pay for a professional community organizer possessing a systemic perspective and team building experience to come in and facilitate a community-wide quality improvement process.

As an increasing number of at least the larger Core facilities became involved in their communities, a model evolved. The local chambers of commerce, unions, and service clubs were responsible for organizing and leading the ongoing familiarization phase. This group worked closely with newspapers and radio and television stations. The educational sector— colleges and secondary schools—took the lead in providing desired training. Courses were offered with mill and Core corporate staff in support. The courses covered general subjects, such as an introduction to the systems approach to quality improvement, and more specific ones, such as organization design and development. The academic sector also provided trouble-shooters.

The growing network of companies with ongoing or new quality improvement processes in place was responsible for helping each other put team networks together. Finally, the long-range-planning exercise was led by a consultant.

While the necessary critical mass had long since been achieved on the corporate level, Core was now anxious to help achieve it on the community level. Other major corporations, impressed by the profits that Core was enjoying, began developing the same systemic perspective. As a result, they, too, became more effectively involved in community efforts to upgrade the overall quality of life.

IDEALIZING, BUT NOT FANTASIZING

All of the pieces discussed above as necessary to a corporate quality improvement process are in place in more progressive Japanese, European, and U.S. firms, though they are not usually as well integrated as they should be. What has been proposed, therefore, is quite possible and logical if our ultimate objective is truly to improve performance and profitability.

Community-wide efforts, too, have been mounted. Yet unfortunately, most have foundered, for many of the same reasons that most corporate quality improvement efforts have thus far foundered. Leaders have not understood the magnitude of the desired undertaking and the need for a systemic perspective. Initial emphasis has been on training or the introduction of statistical measurement techniques rather than on familiarization and team building as a means of rapidly getting people involved and fostering the necessary commitment.

The powers in the community have not been able to agree on one approach. These same people have decided that they are capable of putting the necessary pieces in place themselves rather than seeking professional assistance. Communities have become bogged down in defining what currently exists rather than concentrating on what *ought* to exist. They have become bogged down in developing success measurement tools before they have anything to measure.

The more successful community efforts that I am familiar with, such as the project in Jamestown, New York, and the Mantua project in Philadelphia, have characteristics in common with those of successful corporate and unit efforts. These include:

1. A strong leader or unified group of leaders.
2. A systemic rather than piecemeal perspective.
3. Professional assistance in defining and emplacing the appropriate approach and vehicle.
4. Up-front involvement of all key stakeholder groups in order to take advantage of their expertise and to gain their commitment.
5. An integrated network of project teams that facilitates the necessary free flow of communication.

6. Process ground rules agreed to by everyone.
7. Participative development of a plan for the community's future into which all other process pieces are eventually fit.

PART 3

Obstructions and Opportunities: So Near and Yet So Far

Upon his return to the swamp, following a long and arduous quest, one of our society's more popular philosophers, Pogo, made a pronouncement that could be interpreted as one of the most important and least well understood truisms of the quality improvement movement. He said that he had finally succeeded in finding the enemy and that, sure enough, "they is us."

Sociotechnical theory is a critical component of the systems approach. Its central theme is that technical and management systems development are inseparable. This means that possession of the most efficient manufacturing technology available does not insure success. Until the management system supporting it is equally well thought out, the potential of the technical system will not be realized. Failure will remain a possibility if not an eventual probability.

This truism also describes the relationship between quality improvement efforts and management's attitude. You can offer the most comprehensive approach to quality improvement available, but unless management is willing to accept its new role, the approach will produce no lasting changes.

In Part 1, I have presented a conceptual approach to quality improvement based on systems theory. In Part 2, I have offered the history of the successful implementation of this approach at two of Core Corporation's largest pulp and paper mills.

In Part 3, then, I plan to discuss three major cultural obstructions to the implementation of a successful QIP, not only on the individual corporation level but also on the national level, and how these can be turned into opportunities.

The obstructions that I shall address are the senior management systems of corporations, unions, and academia.

It is becoming increasingly obvious that despite the rhetoric, despite the posturing, a large percentage of upper-level managers, both corporate and union, are having difficulty dealing with the transition to a quality-oriented culture and with the changes that such a transition requires in their own personal styles.

However, it is also increasingly apparent that the members of this group are victims as well as culprits. Their inability to accept the inevitability of change results at least partially from the lack of vision and of team spirit demonstrated by the leaders of another key sector, academia.

In this section, I shall attempt to identify the producers of the reactive (as opposed to proactive) thinking found in these three management groups. I shall show how the three sectors involved are themselves a system, how they interact, and how positive change in one is dependent on and will encourage positive change in the others as we strive to reach our goal of improved quality, not only in our working lives but in our lives in general.

CHAPTER 13

The Corporate Elite Versus Quality

GOOD GUY, BAD GUY

The major in-house roadblock to mounting a comprehensive quality improvement process has been defined by many as middle managers. Middle management sees its ranks being thinned as the hierarchy is collapsed to improve communication. It sees traditional decision-making authority being given to hourly employees. It feels threatened and resists.

Middle managers can, indeed, be an obstacle to an effective QIP, but this can be overcome if employment security is insured and if their new role as facilitators and change agents is properly presented and reinforced. Yet the most serious obstacle is not middle management but senior management, the people upstairs who kicked it all off and who appear periodically to make well-crafted speeches stressing the fact that "improved quality requires cultural change and must become a way of life."

The trick, of course, is to watch their feet as well as their mouths. Employees do just that and learn all too frequently that upper-level managers are indeed for improved quality and the necessary changes, but only so long as they themselves are not affected, only so long as alterations in their own styles of management are not necessary. They have neither the inclination nor the time. They are currently involved in too many crises upon which the fortunes of the company depend to worry about changing the way that they do things.

When upper-level managers feel this way, failure is usually assured. The effort might drag on for years and produce some noteworthy results, but ultimately it will not meet expectations. If the top people don't set the example and play by the rules, no one else will. If the top people decide that they are allowed to modify the rules to deal with the pressures of leadership, others will quickly follow suit.

QUANTIFICATION VERSUS QUALITY IMPROVEMENT

Top-level executives have both long- and short-term objectives when they invest in a QIP. The long-term objective is to steadily improve the corporation's bottom line through better planning, relevant training, the introduction of appropriate statistical measurement tools, and better use of employee expertise. The short-term objective is to enhance the company's image by publicly hyping its new dedication to quality improvement.

Unfortunately, too many of those who start out with both long- and short-term intentions end up focusing on the latter. They become more interested in creating the *image* of improved quality than in actually improving it. This happens because the executives realize that they do not possess a comprehensive enough perspective to engineer what is necessary to positively impact the bottom line through quality improvement.

One reason that they do not possess the necessary perspective is that a majority of them are quantitatively oriented. They are finance people, accountants, engineers, and lawyers. To be more exact, according to "The Corporate Elite" in *Business Week*'s special issue of October 21, 1989, the CEOs of the top 1,000 corporations include 260 finance or accounting experts, 192 engineers/technical experts, and 118 lawyers.[1] Many of these people are most comfortable when they can reduce things to numbers: return on investment, cash flow, staffing levels, working capital, return on net assets, and so on.

The above helps explain why Deming's quantitative tools were so quickly adopted by so many as the all-inclusive answer to quality improvement, while the rest of his message was ignored. It explains why I recently saw on the walls of a corporate headquarters posters announcing that "productivity is simply a matter of the right numbers" and was told that the CEO himself had boiled down the entire quality improvement effort to this one line. Finally, it explains why so many executives think it necessary to invest sizable amounts of effort and money up front in the development of quantitative tools to measure QIP success when experience has proven such tools largely unreliable and unnecessary.

SHARING THE BLAME

Executives who lack the necessary perspective have not been properly trained. Executive training comes from four sources—colleges and universities, in-house programs, consultants, and on-the-job coaching. Despite the growing chorus of pleas from both private and public sectors, most of academia continues to focus on enhancing quantitative and other technical skills. Those necessary to developing employee potential, to integrating employee efforts, and to achieving an effective overview of the total operation and how it fits into the economic, political, and social environment of which it is a part are too frequently ignored or skimmed over.

In-house training and consulting packages can be of value but are too limited in duration and scope to insure the necessary changes in attitude and habit. On-the-job coaching by bosses should provide most of what is necessary. A majority of bosses, however, have not been adequately trained themselves, or are too busy, or see their reports as competitors and shy away from sharing expertise.

A second reason that quantity-oriented executives frequently do not possess the necessary perspective has to do with the pressure that the financial world places on corporations. The head of the organization is ultimately responsible for divining the pending impact of environmental forces and for preparing the organization to profit from that impact. In order to do so, the CEO needs to keep an eye on both the environment and the organization. Ideally, the CEO can concentrate on the organization as a whole, while different parts of that organization monitor and make recommendations concerning environmental forces.

The snag is that the U.S. industrial sector is supported mainly by stock investments handled by brokerage firms whose customers are interested primarily in short-term gain. CEOs are too frequently forced to pay a disproportionate amount of personal attention to this one segment of the external environment. The situation has been made worse by the threat of corporate raiders. As a result, boards of directors lean toward candidates with financial expertise and insist that their CEOs pay close attention to what is happening in financial centers. Such expectations add to the quantity-oriented executive's strength and help excuse the lack of attention to the in-house, nonquantifiable issues.

NECESSARY CHANGES

Taking the above into account, we cannot fault top-level executives entirely for their quantitative orientation and for their failure to understand and play the role necessary to a successful QIP. Academia is partially responsible. Academicians must begin thinking in terms of quality. They must make their educational offerings better fit customer needs. Their shortcomings and those of their programs, at both the undergraduate and higher levels, have been well documented. They must begin listening more carefully and reacting more positively.

Wall Street needs work, too. Brokers are often too engrossed in their own reality, one strictly of numbers, devoid of the faces and emotions necessary to improve quality. Too many aggressive and avaricious financial predators are popping up. Too many intelligent and highly creative young men and women are sitting in their chrome and glass towers trying to figure out ways to beat the system, legally or illegally, in order to impress each other. Life for too many on Wall Street is an "in-group" competition divorced from the reality that it creates elsewhere.

Finally, the big-time money manipulators are hurting the quality improvement movement badly. Leverage and other types of buyouts can be effective quality-enhancing tools in poorly managed companies frustrated by bureaucracies or frozen by tradition. But the new owners must be willing to make the necessary changes and to follow through. Most of today's takeover artists have shown no such willingness.

MANAGEMENT'S ACHILLES HEEL

Another important reason that too many top executives are the main roadblock to successful quality improvement efforts is their inability to function as team players. They might talk about "their" team and go through the motions of seeking input from reports but most decisions are ultimately based on their own intuition or judgment.

This characteristic is well documented by Robert Lefton and V. R. Buzzotta in their article "Teams and Teamwork: A Study of Executive-Level Teams," which appeared in the winter 1987–88 issue of *National Productivity Review*. The authors examined 26 top-level corporate teams, 20 of which were guiding organizations in the Fortune 500 Club. They found little effort at real communication, little listening, a lot of grandstanding, a lot of turf battles, little participative decision making, and little interest in the problems of implementation.

Another indication that many top-level executives are not team players is that they pay themselves too much and refuse to tie their compensation to the bottom line. Measurements of the reasonableness of executive compensation include comparison of the yearly increase with return on the average shareholder equity, comparison with corporate profits, and comparison with the increases that other executives in the same and other industries receive. It is difficult to find a model that incorporates a comparison with what a range of employees in the same company makes.

In terms of tying compensation to the bottom line, we have all read about companies that are not doing well, in which no annual compensation increase was offered or everyone was forced to take a cut. Everyone, that is, except the top-level executives, who found reason to award themselves bonuses or salary increases. Such moves do not foster loyalty to the organization, to the team, or to a quality improvement effort. As one of my students recently wrote:

> During the last two years our company's main industry has been extremely competitive and margins have been sacrificed for market share. Since, during this time, our share of the market has not grown appreciably, upper level management has been forced to initiate other steps to improve the bottom line. One such step has been the elimination of merit increases. During this same period our upper level managers have received record high bonuses, a strategy which has not delighted too many employees. It would seem reasonable to cut back on these bonuses or to eliminate them entirely, as the involved individuals already receive 10–20 times the salary of the average employee. A compensation system that ties every employee's share to the bottom line would improve employees' perception of the fairness of the system.

Actually, the 1:10 or 1:20 ratio cited does not even come close when referring to the compensation received by a growing number of CEOs. The authors of an article in the May 1, 1989 edition of *Business Week* entitled "Is the Boss Getting Paid Too Much?" surveyed 254 companies and found the average CEO's compensation in these companies to be 93 times that of the average hourly worker.[2] The rationale supporting such a high level of compensation is threefold:

1. The CEO works harder and makes more difficult and more critical decisions than everyone else.

2. This high level of compensation is needed to attract and to keep superior talent at the top.

3. In order to protect the company's image, the CEO's pay level must remain competitive with or exceed that of other companies in the same industry.

ANOTHER VIEWPOINT

In terms of the first argument, if the CEO works harder than anyone else, it's because that person is not a team player and feels the need to make all the decisions. A good "manager" doesn't. A good manager gets the right people in the right positions, supports them in their efforts, and helps integrate their decisions. The person that we're talking about, then, is a "boss" rather than a manager and has only him or herself to blame for the fact that the company seems unable to progress beyond crisis management.

In terms of the second argument, there's little value in having the best and the brightest at the helm making decisions if those below, those responsible for implementation, feel disgruntled and are saying, "Let the person who's making all the money solve the problems."

In terms of the third argument, the relationship between the extremely high compensation level of some CEOs and the company's image is not necessarily a positive one. The current rash of articles in major magazines questioning the value of such packages provides evidence of the doubt in the public mind. The people who care the most, of course, are the company's employees. They generally see the "comparable worth" rationalization exactly for what it is and wonder how the CEO finds the nerve to ask them to be less selfish.

MORE LESSONS FROM ABROAD

Top-level executives who understand the need to mount successful QIPs but continue to pay themselves too much and refuse to tie their compensation in any way to the bottom line still have hard lessons to learn from the same Europeans and Japanese who helped convince us of the need for improved quality in the first place.

According to Jan Wessels, the deputy consul general of the Netherlands in New York City, the ratio of CEO pay to that of the average factory worker with 10 years of experience in industrialized Western European nations is between 8:1 and 9:1 before taxes. If the average employee is making $20,000 per year, the CEO is making between $160,000 and $175,000, instead of close to $2,000,000 as in the United States.

According to Japanese managers contacted by David Sulz, currently on the staff of the Wharton Japan Program, this ratio lies between 12:1 and 17:1 with new hourly employees in Japan. Also, according to an article by Katsusada Hirose in the July 1, 1989 issue of *The Japanese Economic Foundation Journal of Japanese Trade and Industry* entitled "Corporate Thinking in Japan and the U.S.," when profits fall, Japanese executives and board members, as leaders, are more willing to punish themselves than are U.S. executives; they are more willing to ask the workers' forgiveness and to take the initial compensation cuts. For example, according to *The Japan Economic Journal*, December 20, 1986, because of losses resulting from poor overseas ventures, Fujitec Corporation slashed executive salaries by 10 to 50 percent. According to the *Japanese Times*, December 31, 1987, Nikko Securities cancelled a planned yearly pay raise for executives because a financial deal had gone sour and the company wanted those responsible to "search their souls." According to the *Nikkei News Bulletin*, April 4, 1986, Mitsubishi Electric, Fujitsu, Toshiba, and Sansui Electric all cut board members' salaries. Exports were lagging due to the growing strength of the yen, and profits were down.

THE RIGHT WAY

Another characteristic of too many top-level executives is that they do not believe in sharing the rewards of improved quality with the employees who have contributed to the involved improvements. Their argument is that if employees are paid a competitive wage and are given decent benefits, it is their responsibility to do the best that they can for the company and to expect nothing extra in return. The problem with distributing a part of additional profits is that employees will begin to expect such rewards whether the company does well or not. Also, the unions will immediately attempt to turn such gift giving into a precedent and negotiate it as a permanent part of the contract.

In contrast, European, Japanese, and U.S. firms seriously interested in improving quality eventually tie everyone's compensation to the bottom line. Everyone who contributes gains a share of the increased profits generated. This share can be in the form of pay raises, bonuses, profit sharing, gain sharing, gifts of stock, or employee stock ownership plans. No matter what form it takes, however, it is an essential ingredient.

One reason that some U.S. companies have soured on the sharing of profits is that they have introduced their plan at the beginning of a QIP as a means of stimulating interest rather than waiting and delivering it as a reward for impressive bottom-line improvements. The results of this strategy have been poor.

Successful QIPs generally follow a pattern. The first phase answers the questions "Why a QIP?" "What's the purpose of the team network?" "What kind of training can we expect?" "What's the role of planning in all this?" It generates curiosity, skepticism, and some enthusiasm in the work force. During the team building and training phases that come next, workers and supervisors get excited about the fact that they have been given the authority to recommend, design, and implement improvements. This excitement is reward enough initially and is supplemented by the more cooperative atmosphere engendered.

In the following months, the payoff becomes the steady improvement seen in overall productivity and in the bottom line. Everyone enjoys being on a winning team. Eventually, however, QIP participants on all levels begin thinking and saying, "Hey, we've helped improve the fortunes of this company. We should share in the financial rewards."

It is at this point, then, that the customized plan should be introduced. Such timing will further heighten employee morale and give a boost to the process. If structured right, it will also provide an ongoing incentive. For example, I have never heard of flagging interest in improved quality at Lincoln Electric, the much-talked-about Cleveland-based manufacturer of arc welding equipment and induction motors, where, according to the article "This Is the Answer" in the July 5, 1982 issue of *Forbes*, employment is guaranteed for those with two years or more of service and where up to 50 percent of yearly compensation frequently arrives in the form of a bonus based on performance.

CULTURAL CHANGE

We have all heard abut the need for cultural change if we are to achieve improved quality. Only now, however, are we beginning to realize the full implication of this pronouncement. Yes, the workplace has to grow more participative and less authoritarian. But sectors external to the corporation that indirectly but significantly impact the nature of the workplace must also change. Academia has to realize that it can better define customer needs if it includes the customer in the process. It must begin thinking of itself as a member of the team. The financial community must be made more responsible and less self-absorbed.

The people with the power to engineer these large-scale societal changes are our top-level executives. But in order to do so successfully, many must first work on their own image. They must achieve a more balanced quantitative/qualitative perspective. They must become real team members. They must be willing to tie their fortunes to the bottom line along with those of their employees.

Only then, bolstered by the support that the team atmosphere provides, will corporate leaders realize their true potential and power. Only then will they become capable of fostering the desired cultural change, both within the workplace and outside. Only then will the quality improvement that they advocate have a chance of becoming a nationwide reality.

NOTES

1. "The Corporate Elite," *Business Week* (October 21, 1989): 28.
2. "Is the Boss Getting Paid Too Much?" *Business Week* (May 1, 1989): 46–48.

CHAPTER 14

Unions Rethink Their Role

OFF TO A SLOW START

Unions have traditionally led the way toward an improved quality of working life. Historically, they have played a major role in securing the 40-hour work week, child labor laws, minimum wage, protection from injury and harassment, and fringe benefits such as health care, vacations, sick leave, and pensions. In terms of the modern-day quality improvement movement, however, as John Hoerr of *Business Week* wrote in "The Payoff from Teamwork," it is now management that is pushing employees in both union and nonunion plants to accept more involvement.[1]

Several reasons exist for the hesitancy and caution of union leaders. One is that though they have as much to gain in the long run, they are more at risk than CEOs. Specifically, while CEOs can fake commitment to a quality improvement process, union leaders can't. CEOs can be extremely gung ho up front, spend millions on consultants, and mandate the involvement of supervisors and hourly employees. At the same time, however, they can refuse to make the changes in their own styles that are critical to success. CEOs can focus on the image of improved quality while avoiding the content and get away with it, at least in the short run. The work force has little leverage, even when the CEO's lack of commitment becomes obvious. At the same time, board members and stockholders are too far removed to evaluate actions properly. The hype and the bottom line are all that they see, and the bottom line can be manipulated.

Union presidents, on the other hand, are directly responsible to and dependent on those most deeply affected by the work-life changes being advocated. They must be sure that quality improvement is not just a management plot to reduce the union's power, or another efficiency study in sheep's clothes aimed at getting more out of a pared-down work force for less.

Another reason for the relatively slow uptake of unions concerns middle management. CEOs can force superintendents, supervisors, and foremen at least to give the process a chance. Promotions and, in extreme cases, continued employment can be used as incentives. National union leaders, however, cannot apply such pressures to local presidents. The latter are elected from below rather than appointed from above and, in turn, influence the election of national leaders.

At the same time, local union presidents frequently lack the broad perspective of national officers. Their attention is focused on office or shop-floor issues. The fact that we are losing world-market share to cultures that have developed a more supportive labor-management relationship—that the traditional adversarial stance is outdated—can be hard for them to relate to.

JUST CAUSE

National union leaders can apply some pressure but must remember that the presidents and members of their local unions know better than anyone what is really going on behind the quality improvement banners at plants and offices. They are naturally suspicious. They have good reason to be. In the United States, corporate management's history of duplicity in its dealings with labor is well documented. The current trend toward paying closer attention to workers' ideas and needs as a means of enhancing both the quantity and quality of output is nothing new. During the last 30 years, movements in this direction have cropped up periodically, especially during down cycles in the economy.

But while job security has been the number-one prerequisite to success in similar European and Japanese efforts, the U.S. sector, despite its supposed understanding of this critical relationship, is currently undergoing yet another wave of corporate staff cuts. A 1989 American Management Association survey found that 39 percent of the corporations polled had cut staff over the last year and that as many as 45 percent were considering making cuts during the current year.[2]

One reason given in a *Time* article entitled "Where Did the Gung-Ho Go?" for U.S. management's inability or unwillingness to make job security a number-one priority was, curiously enough, the pressure of increased global competition. Others included the desire to avoid unfriendly takeovers; the current, unprecedented level of corporate debt; and pressure to show constant improvement in the bottom line.[3]

Union members see the current cuts in benefits being negotiated, the increasing use of temporary workers with no benefits at all, the increasing use of robots, and the comparatively small amount spent in this country on training to enhance employee skills and opportunities, and they have trouble believing that the purpose of the quality improvement process is to better their situation as well as that of the company.

Moving beyond the shortcomings of corporate management and the financial community, however, the fact remains that:

1. We are, indeed, losing market share because other cultures have developed more cost-effective, quality-producing industries.
2. Increasing numbers of our unprofitable companies are being bought and made profitable by foreigners who send the profits home.
3. If this situation doesn't change, workers and unions as well as management will lose.
4. The QIP vehicle is the best that we have for defining and implementing the changes necessary.

A NEW FACE

Unions have a chance to make the difference. They have the power to help U.S. companies move more rapidly in the right direction. First, however, they need to do some rethinking and reshaping of their own role. They need a new face. The old one is outdated. It no longer attracts the way it once did.

Unions need a new strategy for achieving their ultimate ends. Strikes don't work anymore. Management has developed the legal and economic clout necessary to beat or wait strikes out. As a result, according to the Bureau of Labor Statistics, the number of labor stoppages involving 1,000 or more employees has dropped from an average of 331 per year in the 1950s, to 299 per year in the 1960s, to 269 per year in the 1970s, to 64 in 1984, to 54 in 1985.[4]

The more recent tactics of smearing corporations by spreading stories and by boycotting organizations—banks, suppliers, customers, and so on—that do business with the target are not working either. Such efforts divorce themselves largely from the union's traditional source of power—workers, who explain and demonstrate belief in their causes to the public. They move the action onto the corporate playing field. Union lawyers and public-relations experts trade blows with corporate lawyers and public-relations experts, while those who started the whole thing, those who the interaction is supposed to be about, spend most of their time on the sidelines.

What we have here is a race of sorts. If corporate management continues to lead the way toward comprehensive quality improvement, unions might end up even worse off in terms of declining membership. If unions pick up the pace, however, they can share leadership in one of the most important social and economic movements of modern times.

A growing number of progressive union leaders are realizing this and are demonstrating bursts of speed. Lynn Williams of the United Steel Workers (USW) became a strong advocate of a cooperative labor-management approach to quality improvement.[5] Owen Bieber of the United Auto Workers (UAW) has been quoted as saying, "Unions must be willing to establish joint programs with management on shop floors to staunch the flow of jobs overseas."[6] When asked in an interview with *Pulp and Paper* if unions couldn't take the lead in improving labor relations and working for better quality, Wayne Glenn, president of the United Paper Workers International Union (UPIU), replied:

> We have taken the initiative. We've tried to teach our staff how quality improvement programs can be used for the good of all. We want to keep workers from thinking that the company is trying to undermine the union with these programs.[7]

OTHER SIDE OF THE COIN

At the same time, strong resistance can be found among the followers of all these leaders. Local 1010 USW president, Mike Mezo, said, "We don't think there's any benefit to cooperation. No way will we ever take part."[8] A "New Directions" faction broke away from the UAW majority to fight the cooperative movement, saying, for one thing, that it has done little to insure job security, one of its stated goals.

In 1988, a book entitled *Choosing Sides: Unions and the Team Concept* appeared. The authors' advice was to "just say no." They equated the team concept with "management-by-stress," a subtle effort by those in charge to ease workers into an even more demanding form of Frederick Taylor's efficiency-seeking scientific management.

> Management by stress uses stress of all kinds—physical, social, and psychological—to regulate and boost production. It combines a systemic speedup, "just-in-time" parts delivery, and strict control over how jobs are to be done to create a production system which has no leeway for workers, and very little breathing room.[9]

The authors saw collective bargaining agreements that included the team concept as encouraging:

1. Interchangeability, requiring or inducing workers to learn several jobs.
2. Drastic reduction of job classifications giving management increased control over the assignment of work.
3. Less meaning for seniority.
4. Detailed definition of every step of every job, again increasing management's control.
5. Worker participation in increasing their own workload.
6. More worker responsibility without more authority.
7. An attempt to get away from the "I just come to work, do my job and mind my own business" attitude by showing them how they fit into the whole operation.[10]

Much of what they say is true, but the authors, unfortunately, have defined the quality improvement movement based on their own extreme bias, leaving out the parts proven in most cases to enhance quality of working life. They also say that while responsibility is increasing, decision-making authority is not. If the approach is comprehensive, this is absolutely untrue. The book, however, and its popularity, indicate the level of distrust that has to be overcome in many quarters.

GROUNDWORK

Actually, many of the problems facing union leaders are similar to the ones faced by CEOs. These include: an inflexible, hierarchical union management system; too much bureaucracy; and fear of change on all levels. Most quality consultants would recommend the same steps for union officials interested in improving the effectiveness of their operation that they recommend for corporate executives. These include:

1. Begin a campaign to familiarize membership with the concept of quality improvement as it applies to union management and operations. Stress pushing problem solving and decision making down to lower levels.

2. Develop a team approach to union management complete with ground rules. The teams in the network would be built by region or would represent larger companies. Team membership could cross traditional trade boundaries, if appropriate, as corporate quality improvement process team membership does.

3. Mount, with assistance from academia, a training effort to provide union members with the skills necessary to function effectively in a team-driven atmosphere.

4. Turn national and local leaders into facilitators, teachers, resource generators, and resolvers of intra- and interteam conflicts.

In this new system, regional union teams would need to begin speaking for themselves when arbitrating contracts, instead of relying on the national network. An increasing number of corporations are encouraging a direct interface through labor-management committees and other similar vehicles. If unions are seen as opposing this trend, they will most likely lose more of their following.

Another sacred cow that has to be sacrificed is work rules and job restrictions. According to Peter Drucker, it is exactly those industries most tightly bound by work rules and job restrictions—steel, automobiles, consumer electronics, rubber, and so on—that have done the poorest against foreign competitors.[11] Work rules and job restrictions were developed to protect jobs. At the same time, however, they have made jobs even more repetitive and boring, have allowed employees to realize only a limited portion of their potential, have produced a "team" where members cannot assist or fill in for missing teammates, and, in the end, have proved self-defeating in that the resultant loss of productivity has led to layoffs and shutdowns.

MAYBE MORE POWERFUL THAN BEFORE

The strategy of taking the lead in the quality improvement movement can be a no-lose opportunity for unions. Their traditional concerns—job

security, reasonable pay, safety, improved work environment, and benefits—match those of a systemic quality improvement approach. At the
same time, this strategy will improve their status in relation to that of
corporate management. Unions are the only sector capable to forcing
CEOs to take process-related responsibilities seriously. They have the
hammer necessary to make corporate executives play by the rules instead
of creating their own or changing the rules whenever convenient. That
hammer is access to employees who can document shortcomings combined with access, through the media, to a public increasingly interested
in how our corporations are being managed, or mismanaged.

Blowing the whistle on a CEO who is faking a quality improvement
effort can affect both the company's bottom line and the CEO's career. It
can provide a missing but much needed public service. At the same time,
it can help clarify the union's role as guardian of the customer, the
stockholder, and the nonunion as well as union employee.

The sacrifices that union leaders will have to make to prove their
sincerity in this new role—allowing lower-level teams to negotiate their
own contracts, and softening or doing away entirely with work rules and
job restrictions—should not be a giveaway. Something should be de-
manded in return. Possibilities include: a more equitable salary/bonus/
benefit system that ties everyone's take to the bottom line; and a longer-
term corporate strategic planning perspective.

The division of profits is a hot issue. The public is becoming increasingly incensed over the salaries, bonuses, and benefits that CEOs are
awarding themselves. Unions could throw their strength into an effort to
force CEO rewards back to a sensible level and to tie not only the CEO's
but everyone's take in some way to the long-term bottom line. Such an
arrangement is an integral part of any successful quality improvement
process. Profit sharing, gain sharing, employee stock option plans
(ESOPs), and employee ownership are some of the vehicles that have been
developed. Implementation of these vehicles, however, has not always
been smooth. Top-level management has balked or misrepresented the
facts. Lower-level employees have had difficulty understanding the benefits of such a change, or have interpreted it as another management trick.
Unions, taking advantage of their rapport with workers, could help define
and implement the most appropriate vehicle for each situation.

The second item, our corporate sector's short-term perspective and its
negative consequences, has also received much press. One producer of
this problem is again a reward system that puts emphasis in the wrong
place. A 1982 survey by Hewitt Associates showed that 79 percent of U.S.
firms at that time rewarded executives largely for short-term performance.

Year-end bonuses averaged 47 percent of their salaries.[12] We suspect that these percentages are probably even higher today due to increased pressure from investors to show quick profits.

Long-term strategic planning is one of the phases of a comprehensive quality improvement effort. Unless well-thought-out strategic objectives are defined at the top of organizations, the work done at other levels can be wasted. The executive compensation trend defined above therefore must be reversed. Putting increased amounts of stock in the hands of employees who are more interested in job security than in quick profits that might necessitate the elimination of jobs will help calm the passions of the stock market. It will also relieve some of the pressure on corporate executives. Bonuses can then be restructured to reflect longer-term performance and to insure that management's concern is in the right place.

BEGINNING AT HOME

Meanwhile, on the local level, in their new role as facilitators, unions can help guard against workers innovating themselves out of a job. Because it increases productivity and improves supplier and customer relations, a comprehensive QIP usually ends up causing more people to be hired than fired. Job definitions, however, change. Some jobs disappear. Others are combined. Shortsighted number crunchers cannot be allowed to use these changes as an excuse for layoffs and the subsequent, unreasonable increases in responsibility for those remaining.

Unions must also help protect team participants from the wrath of threatened middle managers. Upper-level managers are sometimes hesitant to step in and stop such harassment. They don't want to further alienate a valuable and loyal middle manager. They feel sorry for Joe or Mary and shrink from further aggravating his or her frustration. They might even secretly agree, allowing the manager to say and do what they can't. Whatever the reason, union representatives can function as watchdogs, helping insure that upper-level management reacts properly to such process-threatening behavior.

Unions can help see to it that quality improvement process participants receive proper training. Team members usually do a good job of identifying their own training needs. However, many corporate training departments have their own agendas and aren't organized to meet needs defined outside those agendas. Unions can either play the advocate for workers and encourage corporate training departments to adapt, or, in conjunction with academia, they can help employees establish their own training programs. Such programs, perhaps, can be interfaced with the ones developed to make union management more participative.

Finally, union leaders can continue to educate themselves and can help educate industrial leaders about the need for a systemic instead of a fragmented or totally lopsided approach to quality improvement

TIME TO MOVE OUT

In summation, the quality improvement movement that some union leaders and members still see as a threat can also be regarded as a tremendous opportunity. What it requires is a new perspective and the willingness to shift priorities. The involved changes will not be easy. If unions can make them, however, they will insure a key future role for themselves in the U.S. manufacturing and service sectors. They will also help hasten a shift from our worn-out, confrontational labor-management posture toward a more comfortable and necessary win-win one.

NOTES

1. John Hoerr, "The Payoff from Teamwork," *Business Week* (July 10, 1989): 56.

2. Amanda Bennett, "Business Takes Out Its Trimming Shears," *Wall Street Journal* (October 5, 1989): 2.

3. Janice Castro, "Where Did the Gung-Ho Go?" *Time* (September 11, 1989): 53.

4. "UAW President Defends Policy of Cooperation," *Los Angeles Times* (June 19, 1989): 2.

5. Louis Rukeyser, "Frustrated Unions Take On Corporate Image—And Smear It," *Los Angeles Times* (August 24, 1989): 59.

6. "United Paper Workers' Corporate Campaign News" (September 1988).

7. "UPIU's Wayne Glenn Discusses His Union's Current Goals," *Pulp and Paper* (May 1985).

8. Hoerr, 58.

9. Mike Parker and Jane Slaughter, *Choosing Sides: Unions and the Team Concept* (Boston: South End Press, 1988), 14.

10. Ibid., 5.

11. Peter Drucker, "Workers' Hands Bound by Tradition," *Wall Street Journal* (August 2, 1988): 2.

12. Thomas Donahue, "Labor Looks at Quality of Work Life Programs," *Journal of Contemporary Business* (May 1982): 121.

CHAPTER 15

Education Joins the Team

CASE OF THE MISSING HAMMER

Of the three sectors most important to the quality improvement movement—business, unions, and education—the third appears to be the most reluctant to make the changes necessary to an effective contribution. Business-school curricula and teaching styles are outdated and frequently counterproductive. But while this fact has been made obvious by books, magazine articles, and presidential commissions, very little has happened.

One problem is the lack of a "hammer." The loss of market share, jobs, profits, and investor and employee confidence are making both corporate and union leadership seek new approaches. Such incentives, however, are generally lacking in academia. It is a world apart, where the refusal to accept reality does not necessarily bring negative consequences, where people who have long since lost their flexibility and desire to adapt retain the power to shape curricula, and where leaders enjoy relatively little clout.

Those most affected, the students—unlike employees and stockholders—have no recourse. No grievance committee exists. Even if one did, it would be of little use. Undergraduates are too new to effectively evaluate the relevance of what they are learning. MBA students are too busy during their brief two-year stint with coursework piled on top of a normal eight-to ten-hour day at the office. They grumble but put in their time, no matter how redundant their studies might be.

THE RATIONALIZATION

Academia's rationalization for ignoring the grumbling is that students do not know what they need, that their input concerning course content would be shortsighted. Such talk, at the graduate level, is unrealistic. The reality of the situation is that colleges and universities have a great number of tenured professors on their faculties who are unwilling to change their ways. These professors are well paid. They have to be used. Their courses, no matter how irrelevant, have to be fit into the curriculum.

The president of a large university recently said that perhaps, realistically, it didn't actually make much difference. Top-level executives took the lead in picking and training their replacements, and there was very little that academia could teach top-level executives about management theory and practice.

His statement was a stunning indictment. A great number of top-level executives need help just like everyone else, and the problem is mainly one of education. Such executives have never been encouraged to develop the overview necessary to their new challenge. They have never been trained to think systemically. They continue to focus on pieces rather than on relationships and the whole. They continue to analyze, never learning to synthesize as well.

The fact that some in academia fail to grasp this fact indicates that they have created their own perhaps more comfortable and less demanding reality and that this reality is largely divorced from the reality of the population meant to be served. It is not that the knowledge necessary to encourage the proper perspective in top-level management is lacking. Academicians have been fostering it right along. The contributions of researchers and teachers like Follet, Likert, Herzberg, Maslow, Thorsrud, Emery, Deming, Juran, Drucker, Ackoff, Trist, and Bennis can be extremely valuable to executives and future executives.

THE REALITY

The problem, therefore, is not a lack of content. Rather, it is the business schools' inability or unwillingness to develop the academic vehicle necessary to present this content properly. The problem is one of management. Business departments are not being managed effectively. Their leaders are not practicing what they should be preaching.

Initially, the MBA was created to give students fresh out of liberal arts colleges with little or no background in business the basics. These basics included technical skills in finance, accounting, production, marketing, human resources, and so on. They allowed students to qualify, at least technically, for entry-level management positions.

As time passed, both the environment and student profiles changed. Today, most MBA enrollees have already taken introductory business courses during their undergraduate years or as part of corporate in-house training programs. Most have also spent four or five years in the workplace and have developed during this time a great deal of technical expertise. Thus, by the time they return for their MBAs, they are no longer entry-level applicants but middle-level managers and are interested mainly in enhancing their managerial skills.

However, most MBA programs have failed to adapt to this new situation. They continue to focus on technical skills, paying only lip service to the managerial side of the coin. Therefore, many of the courses required are, at best, repetitious for students, and, at worst, superfluous.

More specifically, problems stemming from the inability or unwillingness of those managing MBA programs to adapt to changing demands include the following factors.

1. The fact that they continue to place too much emphasis on quantitative skills and too little on "qualitative" or people-related skills—those that encourage commitment and innovative thinking. Concerning this point, the Business-Higher Education Forum says:

> The rigor applied to financial and quantitative techniques can, and should, be applied to people management. Such courses should include the skills of interviewing, coaching, counseling, negotiating, motivating, and discipline.[1]

A *Business Horizons* article entitled "What Are Business Schools Doing for Business?" puts it this way:

> Today the criticism is that business schools are turning out "number crunchers" rather than managers with good judgement and imaginative ideas. . . . It is commonly acknowledged that interpersonal skills are a key competence for managers, but that the contribution of business schools toward the development of such skills is doubtful.[2]

2. The fact that while management training programs at both the undergraduate and graduate levels are good at producing technicians, very

few instill the ability to integrate what is critical to good management. They do not encourage a systemic perspective. If anything, they encourage the opposite. They very rarely talk about how the parts of an effective organization should fit together.

The article "What Are Business Schools Doing for Business?" cites both the Ford and Carnegie Reports on this issue, discussing the need for:

> ... achievement in terms of developing imaginative, competent, and flexible managers equipped to deal with the unsolved problems of tomorrow. . . . . Being imaginative in business means having the ability to visualize systemic interconnections among business events and to think counterfactually, that is, to see things not as they are, but as they might be. . . . The key decisions in business are non-programmed and often multidisciplinary.[3]

In "The Failure of Business Education—And What to Do About It," Edward J. Mandt writes:

> To be blunt, the typical business school curriculum fails to prepare students properly. It fills the student's head with facts—accounting facts, economic facts, marketing facts—and specialized theory, such as "management policy and strategy" or "management behavior and organization theory." But none of this is integrated into any kind of cohesive system.[4]

3.   MBAs and the business community have not developed the kind of relationship upon which effective business education should be based. The role of business leaders as university trustees is mainly to help raise money. It is not to contribute to curriculum development or to offer experience and expertise as a classroom resource. According to "What Are Business Schools Doing for Business?," communication between business academics and the business community "appears to be minimal, and perhaps even threatening to both parties."[5]

4.   MBAs do not adequately prepare students to deal with the marketplace environment, especially the international one. They are not preparing our managers to deal effectively with competitors from other cultures. As Dean Derek F. Abell of IMEDE in Lausanne, Switzerland, says, "Over the next decade, a few top European-based schools appear better able to develop what companies need—managers with a practical general-management approach and international experience."[6]

The article "The Executive MBA: A New Way to Develop Talent" voices the belief that not even the best U.S. MBA programs are providing their graduates with the two sets of skills essential to success in the modern business world. These are:

1. Skills that allow students to react successfully to international competition and foreign governments.
2. Skills that allow students to identify and create new business opportunities both at home and abroad.[7]

TIME FOR CHANGE

The most obvious way to deal with the shortcomings defined above is for management program administrators to start listening to the customer and adapting. What they will hear is that a more systemic approach is necessary. At the undergraduate level, this approach should concentrate on developing both the appropriate breadth of perspective and the basic technical skills. Students interested in a management major should be encouraged to take courses in the following business-related areas:

- philosophy/logic (traditional tools for improving thought processes)
- economics
- science (to develop a better understanding of what is possible technologically)
- modern-day ethical/environmental issues
- applied creativity as in painting, writing, and crafts (to foster individuality and the ability to contribute creatively)
- public speaking/writing (effective communication is a key to successful management)
- psychology
- computing/word processing
- statistics

Most of these courses are part of a traditional liberal arts core curriculum. In terms of the business major itself, students should be required to take introductory courses in management and organization theory, finance, accounting, marketing, production, and human resources. These courses will provide the necessary frame of reference. Students should then have the opportunity to take two or three additional electives in one or more of these areas. Anything beyond this would probably be a waste.

Most corporations prefer to provide the bulk of the technical training required by employees themselves, relating it directly to their own operation.

After the undergraduate degree is earned and students move into the work world, a selection of courses should be offered to give them a chance to further improve technical skills before going on for their MBA. They should be allowed to take as many of these courses in as many areas as desired. One of the advantages of waiting until they are employed to enroll in these "advanced" specialization courses is that their schoolwork can be tied more closely to their actual job responsibilities. At the same time, students will be more capable of making useful suggestions concerning course content.

ONWARD AND UPWARD

In terms of an MBA program, high GMAT scores, especially on the quantitative side, should no longer be the most critical prerequisite to acceptance. The applicant's grade performance at the undergraduate and intermediate levels should be considered, but his or her record as an employee should be given greater weight. At least two recommendations should be required from bosses stating that the applicant is managerial material. This would avoid students' wasting time and money when the company has no plans to move them into a higher-level management position. It would also help force performance issues to the surface, which, until this point, had been avoided.

The MBA program based on systems theory should offer courses on three levels. The first concerns interaction between individuals and between members of groups. The second concerns the organization as an integrated system. The third concerns the environment in which the organization must function, both domestic and, increasingly, international.

Courses developed to meet first-level needs should teach interpersonal and group management skills—communication, counseling, problem solving, group process, motivation, and so on. Those developed to satisfy second-level requirements should give the student an idea of how the pieces of organizations should and do fit together, of the various ways that systems dealing with production, decision making, incentives, problem solving, planning, communication, and so on can and should complement each other. Finally, the courses developed to satisfy third-level requirements should offer students an idea of how the organization as a whole fits into the larger environment of which it is a part—the industry, the marketplace, the relevant realms of technology, the community, the nation, the world.

Based on the above, MBA-program core courses should include:

- An Introduction to Systems Theory and the Systems Approach to Management
- Organization Behavior (employee level)
- Strategies for Making Employees More Productive (work group level)
- The Management and Integration of Key Organization Systems (organization level)
- Organization Planning (organization level)
- Economic Trends and Their Effects on Organization Policy (environmental level)
- Political, Legal, and Social Trends and Their Effects on Organization Policy (environmental level)

Prerequisites to the MBA should be courses insuring adequate understanding in the key areas of technical expertise. These courses could be taken at the undergraduate level, during the period between undergraduate and graduate study, or at the beginning of the MBA. Concerning students who believe that their work experience has provided an adequate conceptual and practical background in one of these areas, a competency examination could be administered and the student exempted if he or she passes.

AND NOW FOR STYLE

Whereas the problems of undergraduate and graduate management curricula are at least being identified and discussed, those regarding style are receiving almost no attention at all. Reorienting the thinking of bosses who have fought their way up through the ranks and have been doing things the same way for 30 years can be an extremely difficult task. Newer managers tend to be less cynical, less defensive, and more willing to try something new. These, then, are the people who are going to show the way, maybe not tomorrow, but in the next 10 to 20 years. They are also the people that we have sitting in MBA classrooms, reading Ouchi, Peters, Naisbitt, and Pinchot and discussing the corporate world's current and growing emphasis on quality, on discouraging in-house competition, on encouraging teamwork, on pushing decision making down, and on getting employees more involved in shaping their own reality.

But while they may be reading these books and discussing these concepts, the young managers are rarely experiencing the new atmosphere being described. The traditional MBA classroom situation pretty much mirrors the traditional workplace. The relationship between the professor (manager) and students (workers) is adversarial. The professor (manager) makes all the important decisions without input from the students (workers). The students (workers) are responsible to the professor (manager) for completing a certain quantity and quality of work during a predefined period of time. Their reward is based on their production level. A strict hierarchy exists. Bounds of authority are well marked and guarded. Team efforts are relatively rare, and students (workers) are in no way responsible for helping improve their classmates' (coworkers') performance. In fact, they are usually in competition with classmates (coworkers) and can excel only at their expense because the teacher (manager) is grading (paying) on a curve; because only so many *A*s ($10), *B*s ($5), and *C*s ($1) will be awarded.

Thus, no matter what materials are being presented, the traditional MBA classroom situation is reinforcing by example the old, competitive, hierarchical, adversarial, mechanistic mode of interaction. It is like a parent who smokes a cigarette while lecturing children on the evils of smoking. It is hypocritical. When professors or MBA program administrators say that the traditional approach to teaching has lasted this long because it is the best, we are reminded of the old-time supervisor who makes all the decisions and tells workers not to try to think but just to do their jobs: "Because that's the way things have always been done around here."

A QUALITY-SEEKING APPROACH

Academicians should stop reinforcing the old-style values in the classroom and begin introducing those of the quality-seeking workplace. Specifically, they should begin encouraging a more participative atmosphere. They should start sharing their procedural decision-making responsibility and power. The essence of this new atmosphere should be the team approach.

For example, at the beginning of the semester, the MBA course professor could present an outline of topics to be covered along with the basic text and a list of required readings. The professor might then announce that students, from that point on, would run the class. As we have said, a majority of MBA candidates now hold full-time jobs. Therefore, all have undergraduate training, and most have job experience from which to draw. Teams could be formed. Each could pick a topic or topics, research them, present them, and lead the discussion. These teams, in effect, could be encouraged to function like autonomous work groups, responsible to the manager (professor) for the final results but in control of their own activities.

Teams could be required to provide their own presentation materials. They could be encouraged to bring in actual problems from the workplace around which to build presentations. The professor (manager) could function as a facilitator, encouraging, helping generate requested information, keeping check on team preparations to make sure that members do not wander too far off track, fleshing out presentations when necessary, reviewing and stressing key points, helping coordinate team efforts to avoid overlap, and taking the lead in tying the presentations together into a meaningful whole. This, of course, is exactly the role that managers play in companies with successful quality improvement processes.

TEAM REWARDS

Just as all members of an autonomous work group receive the same salary and bonus, all members of the presentation team should receive the same grade. The complaint occurs that some students will do more work than others. However, this situation also arises in the workplace. It is one of the realities that managers must learn to deal with. Again, the team could function like an autonomous work group. At the beginning of the course, the professor could announce that noncontributing members can be dropped from teams by vote. If the "dropped" student (worker) is not accepted by another team (work group), the professor (manager) could also have the right to drop (fire) that student (worker) from the class (company).

Presentation grades should be based in part on style—on the creativity of the presentation and on the amount of class participation achieved. This would discourage verbatim readings from the text and other resources while encouraging students to support each other's efforts. Teams could put on plays, sponsor "friendly" competitions between class members, demonstrate new techniques with the aid of outside experts, or show homemade videos. Presentation grades should count at least as much as exam grades toward the final grade.

Generally, this approach would tend to raise the class average. Yet emphasis at the MBA level should be on insuring that students get the most for their time and money, rather than on ranking them. A safe guess would be that a majority of companies are much more interested in the new and enhanced skills and knowledge that employees bring home than in whether they received an *A* or a *B*, whether they ranked first in their class or twenty-fifth. The ideal grading system from this viewpoint would, of course, be a simple pass-fail one.

EVERYONE BENEFITS

In summary, then, the advantages of modeling the MBA class after the "new world" workplace include the following:

1. Students will learn the advantages of a team effort.
2. Rather than trying to beat each other, students will concentrate on learning as much as they can from each other.
3. The classroom experience will help shape positive workplace habits and attitudes.
4. Variety in presentational styles will help make the course more interesting.
5. Students will get a chance to practice presenting themselves and controlling a session.
6. The professor will frequently learn something new and, at the same time, will suffer less chance of burnout.

One final comment is necessary. It concerns undergraduate management programs as opposed to MBA programs. Because students at the undergraduate level frequently lack relevant previous academic training and job experience, it is necessary for professors to exercise more control over both course content and style. However, it is also important to introduce the team approach to learning at this level so that students can carry the seeds of change along with them when they graduate and enter the full-time work force. This introduction can be accomplished, perhaps, in a preliminary, nonquantitative course such as "Management and Organization Theory."

BUT WHAT ABOUT THE HAMMER?

A number of ways to improve college and university management education programs has been suggested. The question is, how do we force business department faculty and administrators to budge from their usually defensive posture and pay more attention?

Many consider the major problem to be the aforementioned tenure, a system created originally to insure the academic freedom that professors require for unrestricted inquiry and research, and to make teaching positions more attractive by providing long-term job security. Threats to academic freedom, however, have rarely been a serious issue in this country and have almost always been beaten back. At the same time, the long-term security piece has often caused more damage than good. It has allowed too many academicians to function like irresponsible bureaucrats, going through the motions, expanding as little time and energy as possible, accepting as little responsibility as possible, and risking nothing because the reward is assured so long as the boat is not rocked.

The University of California at Berkeley recently sent shock waves through academia by proposing to scrap its tenure system. Such a move, however, would not be enough. Training is the real issue. College professors spend years, decades, immersed in and teaching one approach to reality. Their interpretation of the world is usually selective and narrow. Very few of them, tenured or not, are capable of a systemic perspective concerning curriculum development. Their immediate interest is in protecting their turf, in making sure that their viewpoint receives the attention that it merits. Department chairman, in turn, are professors who have been promoted. They suffer the same shortcomings that many CEOs possess. They are specialists with little formal management training. As such, they bring to their new jobs a skewed sense of reality that is bound to influence their decisions.

The hammer obviously has to come from outside the department and, due to the power of the tenured set and the academic freedom issue, from outside the institution. Other colleges and universities are not much help. A comparison of the undergraduate and MBA curricula of the top 30 management departments in the country will show very few differences. Everyone is doing pretty well. The number of applicants continues to be greater than the number of slots to be filled. Why risk change, especially when suggesting even slight adjustments to curricula sparks anguish?

THE CUSTOMER MAKES IT WORK

The hammer has to come from even further away. It has to come from the industrial sector. Corporations must get fed up with spending large amounts of money to have employees spend long hours learning things that they already know or that are of questionable value. They have to get over the belief that an MBA diploma with the name Northwestern, or Wharton, or Harvard, or Chicago, or Stanford on it automatically qualifies graduates to be superior managers. They have to get over the misconception that an MBA diploma with some college or university name on it is requisite to advancement beyond certain levels of management.

The diplomas, and the names of institutions of higher learning on them, in many cases, are little more than impression pieces, because the substance supporting them is the wrong substance. Corporations, unions, and other organizations have to start paying closer attention to what employees are actually studying. When they do, and realize, or admit, that, despite the growing body of evidence, the growing chorus of pleas, students are still not being prepared for modern-day management positions, they will do the obvious—develop their own comprehensive management training programs.

One large corporation, a group of small ones, or a corporation-union partnership will develop a curriculum and hire hand-picked professors to come in and teach it. Despite the fact that they will pay these people well, they will end up spending far less for employee education. At the same time, they will be able to constantly adjust and adapt their curriculum, learning from both students and the environment. They will award some type of degree. It will not be recognized by academia, but will quickly prove its value in terms of content and, therefore, will rapidly gain legitimacy and popularity.

Academia will worry loudly about the business sector not having the proper perspective. It might even try to blackball professors willing to teach in these renegade schools. In order to remain competitive, however, MBA programs will finally be forced to begin listening seriously and reacting in the right manner.

Once the dust settles, the end result will most likely be that instead of the business sector surrendering students to the academic sector to be educated however academia sees fit, the two sectors will work together, pooling expertise and resources to insure that students receive the most relevant education possible. The end result will be that management professors become more directly involved in the real world that they are helping to mold. The end result will be that corporate executives and union officials get over their uneasiness around academicians and make better use of their talents. The end result, in sum, will be a win-win, quality-seeking situation from which all sectors profit and learn.

NOTES

1. *America's Business Schools: Priorities for Change: A Report by the Business-Higher Education Forum* (Washington, D.C., May 1985), 3.

2. Roger Dickinson, Anthony Herbst, and John O'Shaughnessy, "What Are Business Schools Doing for Business?" *Business Horizons* (November-December 1983): 46.

3. Ibid., 47.

4. Edward J. Mandt, "The Failure of Business Education—And What to Do About It," *Management* (August 1982): 48.

5. Dickinson, Herbst, and O'Shaughnessy, 51.

6. Derek F. Abell, "Readers Report," *Business Week* (April 14, 1986): 10.

7. George S. Odiorne, "The Executive MBA: A New Way to Develop Talent," *Personnel* (November 1985): 40.

Bibliography

Abell, Derek. "Reader's Report." *Business Week*, April 14, 1986.

Ackoff, Russell L. *Creating the Corporate Future*. New York: Wiley, 1981.

———. "Does Quality of Life Have to Be Quantified?" *General Systems*, 20, 1975.

———. *Management in Small Doses*. New York: Wiley, 1986.

———. "The Mismatch Between Educational Systems and the Requirements for Successful Management." *Wharton Alumni Magazine*, Spring 1986.

———. *Redesigning the Future*. New York: Wiley, 1974.

Alexander, Kenneth. "The Worker, the Union, and the Democratic Workplace." *The American Journal of Economics and Sociology*. October 1987.

Allio, Robert J. "Executive Retraining: The Obsolete MBA." *Business and Society Review*, Summer 1984.

"America's Business Schools: Priorities for Change: A Report by the Business-Higher Education Forum." Washington, D.C.: May 1985.

Avedisian, Joyce, Ron Cowin, Doug Ferguson, and Bill Roth. "Beyond Crisis Management." *Pulp and Paper International*, February 1986.

Batter, William M. "Productivity and the Working Environment." The Wharton School of the University of Pennsylvania Lecture Series, March 17, 1985.

Bennett, Amanda. "Business Takes Out Its Trimming Shears." *Wall Street Journal*, October 5, 1989.

Burck, Charles. "What's in It for the Unions?" *Fortune*, August 24, 1981.

Castro, Janice. "Where Did the Gung-Ho Go?" *Time*, September 11, 1989.

Chems, Albert, and Louis Davis. *The Quality of Working Life*. 2 vols. London: Collier Macmillan, 1973.

"Chrysler Ties Executive Bonuses to Worker Profit-Sharing." *Los Angeles Times*, April 19, 1988.

Commoner, Barry. *The Closing Circle*. New York: Alfred A. Knopf, 1971.
"Company's Courses Go Collegiate." *Business Week*. February 26, 1979.
"The Corporate Elite." *Business Week*, October 21, 1989.
"Developing Managers Not a Corporate Priority." *Wall Street Journal*, April 18, 1988.
Dickinson, Roger, Anthony Herbst, and John O'Shaughnessy. "What Are Business Schools Doing for Business?" *Business Horizons*, November-December 1983.
Dickson, John. "Plight of Middle Management." *Management Today*. December 1977.
Donahue, Thomas. "Labor Looks at Quality of Work Life Programs." *Journal of Contemporary Business*, 6, 1982.
Drucker, Peter. "Worker's Hands Bound by Tradition." *Wall Street Journal*, August 2, 1988.
Emery, Fred, and Einar Thorsrud. *Democracy at Work*. Leiden: Martinus Nijhoff Social Sciences Division, 1976.
Employee Development Review Guidebook. Johnson and Johnson, New Brunswick, N.J., 1978.
Fenwick, P., and E. Lawler. "What You Really Want from Your Job." *Psychology Today*, May 1978.
Geber, Beverly. "Teaming Up with Unions." *Training*, August 1987.
Gharajedaghi, Jamshid. "On the Nature of Development." *Human Systems Management* 4 (1984).
———. *Toward a Systems Theory of Organization*. Seaside, Cal.: Intersystems Publications, 1985.
Hackman, Richard, and Lloyd Suttle. *Improving Life at Work*. Santa Monica, Cal.: Goodyear Publishing, 1977.
Harvard Business School MBA Program 1988. Cambridge, Mass.: Harvard University Press, 1988.
Hirose, Katsusada. "Corporate Thinking in Japan and the U.S." *The Japanese Economic Foundation Journal of Japanese Trade and Industry*, July 1, 1989.
Hoerr, John. "Is Teamwork a Management Plot? Mostly Not." *Business Week*, February 20, 1989.
———. "The Payoff from Teamwork." *Business Week*, July 10, 1989.
———. "Power-Sharing Between Management and Labor: It's Slow Going." *Business Week*, February 17, 1986.
Hofstadter, Richard. *Social Darwinism in American Thought*. New York: George Braziller, 1959.
Holden, Constance. "Innovation: Japan Races Ahead as U.S. Falters." *Science*, November 14, 1980.
Huddleston, Kenneth, and Dorothy Fenwick. "The Productivity Challenge: Business/Education Partnership." *Training and Development Journal*. 37:4 (April 1983).
Hymowitz, Carol. "Employers Take Over Where Schools Fail to Teach the Basics." *Wall Street Journal*, January 22, 1981.
Iacocca, Lee A., with William Novak. *Iacocca: An Autobiography*. New York: Bantam Books, 1984.
"Is the Boss Getting Paid Too Much?" *Business Week*, May 1, 1989.
The Japanese Economic Journal, December 20, 1986.
Japanese Times, December 31, 1987.
Jardim, Anne. *The First Henry Ford: A Study in Personality and Business Leadership*. Cambridge, Mass.: MIT Press, 1970.
Jenkins, David. *Job Power*. Baltimore: Penguin Books, 1973.

Jenkins, Roger L., Richard C. Reisenstein, and F. G. Rogers. "Report Card on the MBA." *Harvard Business Review*, September-October, 1984.

Johnston, Joseph and Associates. *Educating Managers.* San Francisco: Jossey-Bass, 1986.

Kamber, Igor. "Thank Labor for Our High Quality of Life." *Los Angeles Times*, September 4, 1989.

Lefton, Robert, and V. Buzzotta. "Teams and Teamwork: A Study of Executive-Level Teams." *National Productivity Review*, Winter 1987–88.

Lohr, Steve. "Overhauling America's Business Management." *New York Times Magazine*, January 4, 1981.

"Managing, A Study in Neglect." *Los Angeles Times*, May 23, 1988.

Naisbitt, John. *Megatrends.* New York: Werner Books, 1982.

New Manager Transition: A Management Tool. Johnson and Johnson, New Brunswick, N.J., 1931.

Nichols, Don. "Unions Play Catch-up to Today's Work Environment." *Management Review*, February 1988.

Nikkei News Bulletin, April 4, 1986.

Parker, Mike, and Jane Slaughter. *Choosing Sides: Unions and the Team Concept.* Boston: South End Press, 1988.

Performance, Potential, and Development Review Guidebook. McNeil Pharmaceutical, Springhouse, Pa., 1983.

"Rebuilding America: Start at the Factory." *Wall Street Journal*, May 16, 1988.

"Remaking the Harvard MBA." *Business Week*, March 24, 1986.

Renolds, Larry. "Labor's Leaders Changing to Meet the Times." *Management Review*, February 1988.

Roth, William, Jr. "Designing a New Academic Management Training Program." *SAM Advanced Management Journal*, Winter 1988.

———. "Do Safety Programs Really Work?" *Pulp and Paper International*, January 1988.

———. "Dos and Don'ts of Quality Improvement." *Quality Progress*, August 1989.

———. "Five Phases to Success." *Quality and Participation*, June 1989.

———. "Get Training Out of the Classroom." *Quality Progress*, May 1989.

———. "The Great Quality Shell Game." *Personnel*, December 1988.

———. "Keeping the Jungle Out of the MBA Classrooms." *Personnel*, September 1990.

———. "The Missing Hammer." *Quality and Participation*, March 1991.

———. "A New Role for Unions." *Quality and Participation*, September 1990.

———. *Problem Solving for Managers.* New York: Praeger, 1985.

———. "Putting It All Together." *Manufacturing Technology International*, 1991.

———. "Quality: Rebirth of the Systems Approach." *Quality Digest*, January 1991.

———. "Quality Through People: A Hit for HR." *Personnel*, November 1989.

———. "The Second Subtle Link Between Quality and Globalization." *Pulp and Paper International*, March 1991.

———. "Today's MBA: A Lot to Learn." *Personnel*, May 1989.

———. "Try Some Quality Improvement Process Glue." *Quality and Participation*, December 1989.

———. "What's Going On Down in Louisiana?" *Pulp and Paper International*, September 1987.

———. "Why Aren't Leaders Leading?" *Quality and Participation*, June 1991.

————. *Work and Rewards: Redefining Our Work Life Reality*. New York: Praeger, 1989.

Rukeyser, Louis. "Frustrated Unions Take on Corporate Image—And Smear It." *Los Angeles Times*, August 24, 1989.

Taylor, Frederick. *The Principles of Scientific Management*. New York: Harper, 1911.

"This Is the Answer." *Forbes*, July 5, 1982.

Trist, Eric. "The Evolution of Socio-Technical Systems." *Issues in the Quality of Working Life*. No. 2. Ontario: Ontario Ministry of Labor, 1980.

————. "The Quality of Working Life and Organizational Improvement." Unpublished. Management and Behavioral Science Center, The Wharton School, October 1979.

Trist, Eric, G. W. Higgins, H. Murray, and A. B. Pollock. *Organizational Choice*. London: Tavistock Institute Publications, 1963.

"UAW President Defends Policy of Cooperation." *Los Angeles Times*, June 19, 1989.

"UPIU's Wayne Glenn Discusses His Union's Current Goals." *Pulp and Paper*, May 1985.

"The Vision of MITI Policies in the 1980s." Tokyo: Ministry of International Trade and Industry, 1979.

The Wharton School MBA Program Bulletin, 1988–89. Philadelphia: University of Pennsylvania Press, 1988.

"When Companies Tell Business Schools What to Teach." *Business Week*, February 10, 1986.

Yardley, Jonathan. "Should Universities Remain Shelters for the Slothful?" *Los Angeles Times*, January 11, 1990.

Index